quilting UFOs
with helen's hints

HELEN SQUIRE

American Quilter's Society
P. O. Box 3290 • Paducah, KY 42002-3290
www.AmericanQuilter.com

The American Quilter's Society (AQS), located in Paducah, Kentucky, is dedicated to promoting the accomplishments of today's quilters. Through its publications and events, AQS strives to honor today's quiltmakers and their work and to inspire future creativity and innovation in quiltmaking.

Text © 2008, American Quilter's Society
Artwork © 2008 American Quilter's Society

Editor: Helen Squire
Graphic Design: Lynda Smith
Cover Design: Michael Buckingham
Photography: Charles R. Lynch, unless otherwise indicated

American Quilter's Society
P. O. Box 3290 • Paducah, KY 42002-3290
www.AmericanQuilter.com

Additional copies of this book may be ordered from the American Quilter's Society,
PO Box 3290, Paducah, KY 42002-3290, or online at: www.AmericanQuilter.com.

All rights reserved. No part of this book may be reproduced, stored in any retrieval system, or transmitted in any form, or by any means including but not limited to electronic, mechanical, photocopy, recording, or otherwise, without the written consent of the author and publisher. The patterns in this book may be reproduced, resized, copied, and altered for use by the purchaser and their photocopying service. The purchaser has the right to use any of these patterns repeatedly for personal use or in a custom quilting business. The permission does not extend to entering patterns into a digital, computerized automated quilting machine without the express written consent of the author and publisher. The use of any pattern design for promotion or publication purposes, must obtain written permission from author and publisher. The purchaser may not copy or distribute these patterns for monetary gain. Mass production by manufacturers is strictly prohibited.

Library of Congress Cataloging-in-Publication Data

Squire, Helen.
  Quilting UFOs with Helen's hints / by Helen Squire.
     p. cm.
  ISBN 978-1-57432-970-4
  1. Quilting--Patterns. 2. Patchwork--Patterns. I. Title.

TT835.S673 2008
746.46'041--dc22

2008042207

Proudly printed and bound in the United States of America

dedication
To my friend Marian Piehler

acknowledgments

The following quilters generously lent me their unfinished projects so that I might share my quilting suggestions with you, the reader: Pearl Lucey, Cindy Dietrich, Candace Casciano, and Rosemary Hopkins.

Meredith Schroeder, who when she saw me teach a UFO workshop said, "You need to write a book on this subject."

contents

Introduction 4
- Irene • Irene Reversed •

Helen's Hints 5–7

Adapting Patterns 8–11
- Basket Ring • Le Fan •

Design Choices 12–13
- Cindy's Continuous Lines 7½" •

Quilting Principles 14–15
- Canadian Checkerboard •

Vintage Quilts 16–21
- Awesome Square 7½" block • Turkish Square 7½" block •
- Awesome inspired sashing • Updated Fans • Awesome Delight •

Marking Techniques 22–25
- 7" Kaylee's Square • Kaylee's Border •

Structural Quilting 26–29
- Kentucky Star • 4" Rickey Cable • 3" Rickey Cable Border •
- Rickey Cable Design •

Fabric Choices 30–37
- Candace • Virginia Reel Left • Virginia Reel Right •
- Virginia's Corner 1 • Virginia's Corner 2 •
- Virginia Pantograph Horizontal •
- Virginia Pantograph Vertical •
- Hearts and Flowers Border • Radiance 7" Continuous •

Southwestern Quilt Top 38–43
- Warrior Shield • Celestial Variation • Glorified Chain •

Embroidery Inspired 44–49
- Valerie • Valerie Reversed • Maureen • Miss Vickie •
- Valerie's Lace • Valerie's Flower Basket • Valerie's Border •

Freehand Embroidery 50–55
- Embroidered Bird • Redwork Garden Continuous •
- Benjamen 2" Border • Redwork Whimsy Square •
- Redwork Whimsy Block • Whimsy-on-Point •

Botanical Plants 56–63
- Anemone • Iris • Frankincense • Myrrh • Apricot •
- Pomegranate • Flax • Crocus • Olive • Fig •
- Almond • Sweet Storax •

Inspiration 64–69
- Awesome 3" • Bodacious 3" • Creative 2½" • Delightful 2½" •
- Awesome Maze • Awesome Center • Maggie •

Developing a Pattern Series 70–81
- D.C. Delight 5" • Washington Corner 2½" • D.C. Corner 2½" •
- Spun Sugar • Potomac Pantograph • 4" Turkish Border •
- Turkish Border 2 • Delightful Sashing •
- Turkish Delight 6" Circle • Turkish Inspired •
- Turkish Cross • Turkish Sashing •
- Florida Sunset Double Border • Florida Sunset Sashing •
- Gulf Coast • 4" Floridian • Florida Border •
- Florida L Continuous • Florida R Continuous •

Medallions 82–85
- Mandy • Blackburn Medallion • Blackburn Scroll 7½" •

From Hand to Continuous 86–89
- Rose Marie Continuous 2½" • Rose Marie 3" Continuous Corner •
- Rose Marie Square • Ring of Roses •

Worldwide Quilting 90–94
- Geometric Sashing • Pamela's Rhythm • Geometric Sashing 2 •
- Pretty Pamela • Linda • Hari • Laurel • Jane • Kristyn •
- Elizabeth •

About the Author 95

introduction

There is so much to write about UFOs—unfinished quilt objects—and yet, so little has been written! For the last thirty-five years I have taught and lectured on quilting, the art of joining three layers together. Other teachers and authors stress their sewing techniques, color values, fabric selections and manipulations, etc., etc., and then leave students with the dreaded three words: quilt as desired.

I devised my four question formulas to focus on the decisions that govern the quilting choices for every project. Ten UFO quilts and charts are included to provide diverse examples. The forty-five illustrations scattered throughout the over one-hundred quilting patterns showcase details, and the seventeen sub-chapters give a written explanation of my design philosophy.

This is my ninth pattern book suitable for both hand and machine quilters. I talk about adapting patterns, as well as developing a series of designs for borders, blocks, and sashing strips. The pages of patterns inspired by the embroidery samples are my personal favorite while the botanical plants were the most challenging to design.

Did you know that the fabrics you choose to make your quilt have already determined the scale and proportion of the quilting patterns? Examples of design and fabric choices will show you what I mean, while the sub-chapters on structural quilting, marking techniques, and quilting principles will address some well-known facts of quiltmaking.

Since 1997, I have designed and written "Helen's Hints: Creative Quilting Designs" for *American Quilter* magazine. The larger page size of this book allows me to enhance and expand a few of those patterns. Some of my previous books have been converted into CD-ROMs and, surprisingly, outsell the books because of the ease and ability to resize the designs. Look for them at your favorite quilt shop or supply catalogs, or order them directly from the American Quilter's Society, my publisher. As usual, you have my written permission to computer scan or photocopy my patterns and use them for your own quilts. Please refer to the disclaimer on page 2.

The information in Helen's Hints, on the next page, are the "Helen-isms" I teach. They were formatted from my experiences and are so basic I sometimes hesitate to mention them in class—thinking them as obvious—but the light bulbs of understanding always brighten as students say "ah-ha," and nod in agreement.

May you enjoy every stitch in this book.

IRENE

IRENE REVERSED

QUILTING UFOS with *Helen's Hints* • Helen Squire

helen's hints

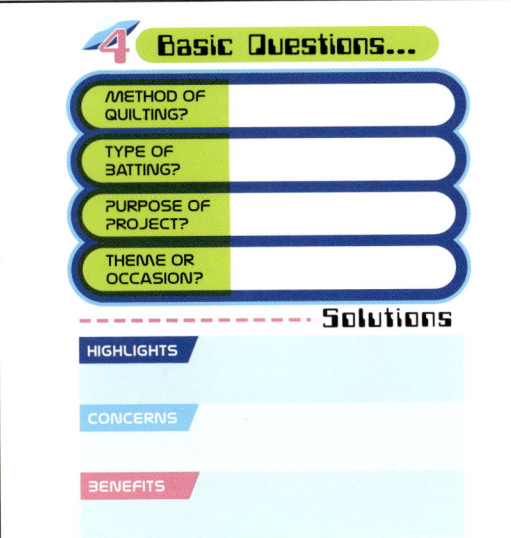

This chart enables you to make sound decisions based on the loft of the batt and if quilted by hand or machine.

The "muslin master" is one-quarter of the pre-planned quilting design plus two inches—which shows what happens at the center of the sides.

Add extra wide seam allowances along all outside edges before you cut. This provides a "fudge" factor when the quilt top shifts.

To prevent sagging, inside narrow borders need some structural quilting across the width, not only quilting-in-the-ditch along the length.

Stop quilting the pre-marked design temporarily along the edges. Square off the corners then resume quilting the full design.

For any adjustments, start "marking" at the 2 o'clock position, never at the corners. It is an inconspicuous place and easily remembered.

QUILTING UFOS with *Helen's Hints* • Helen Squire

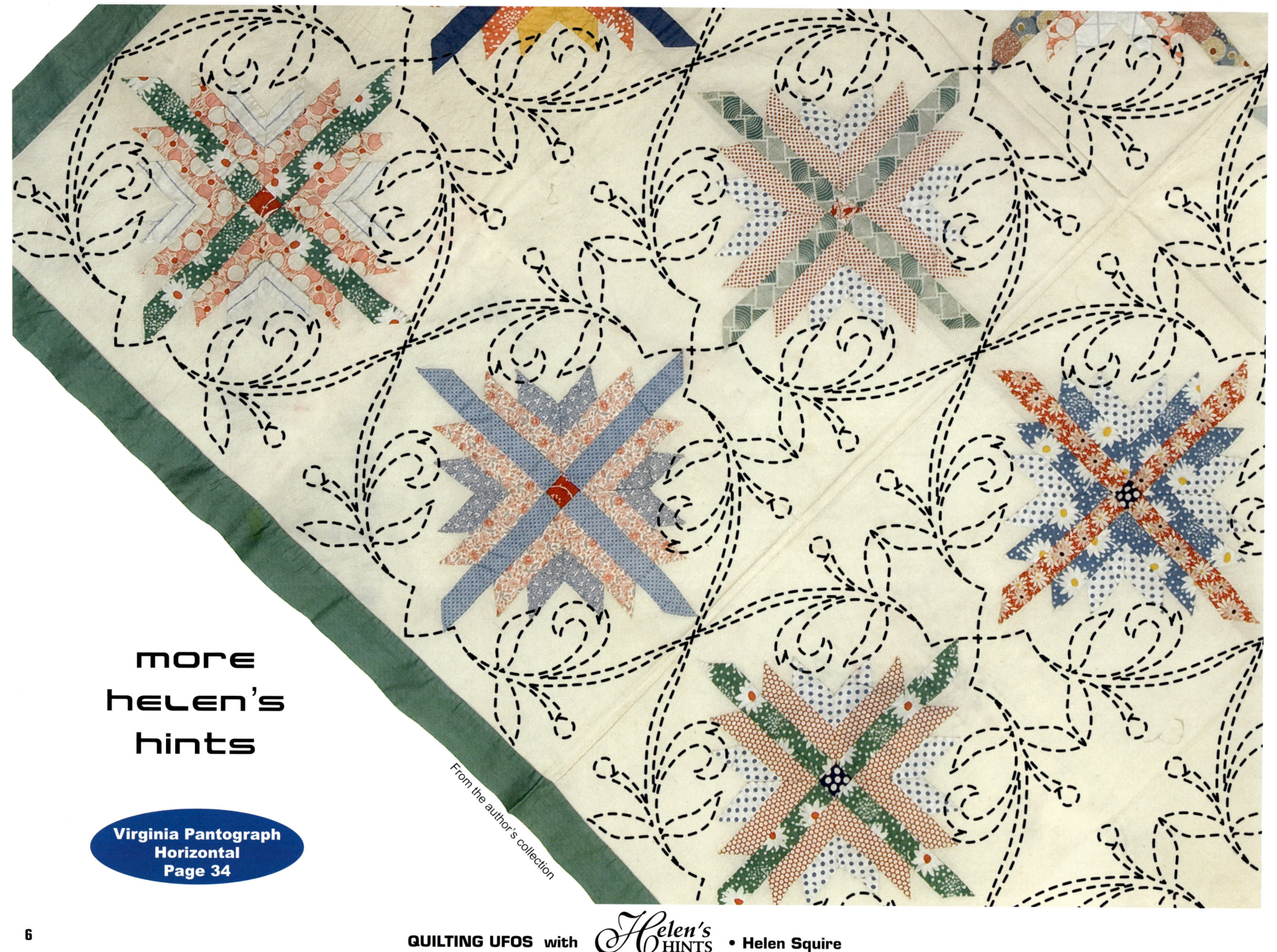

more helen's hints

Virginia Pantograph
Horizontal
Page 34

From the author's collection

6   QUILTING UFOS with *Helen's Hints* • Helen Squire

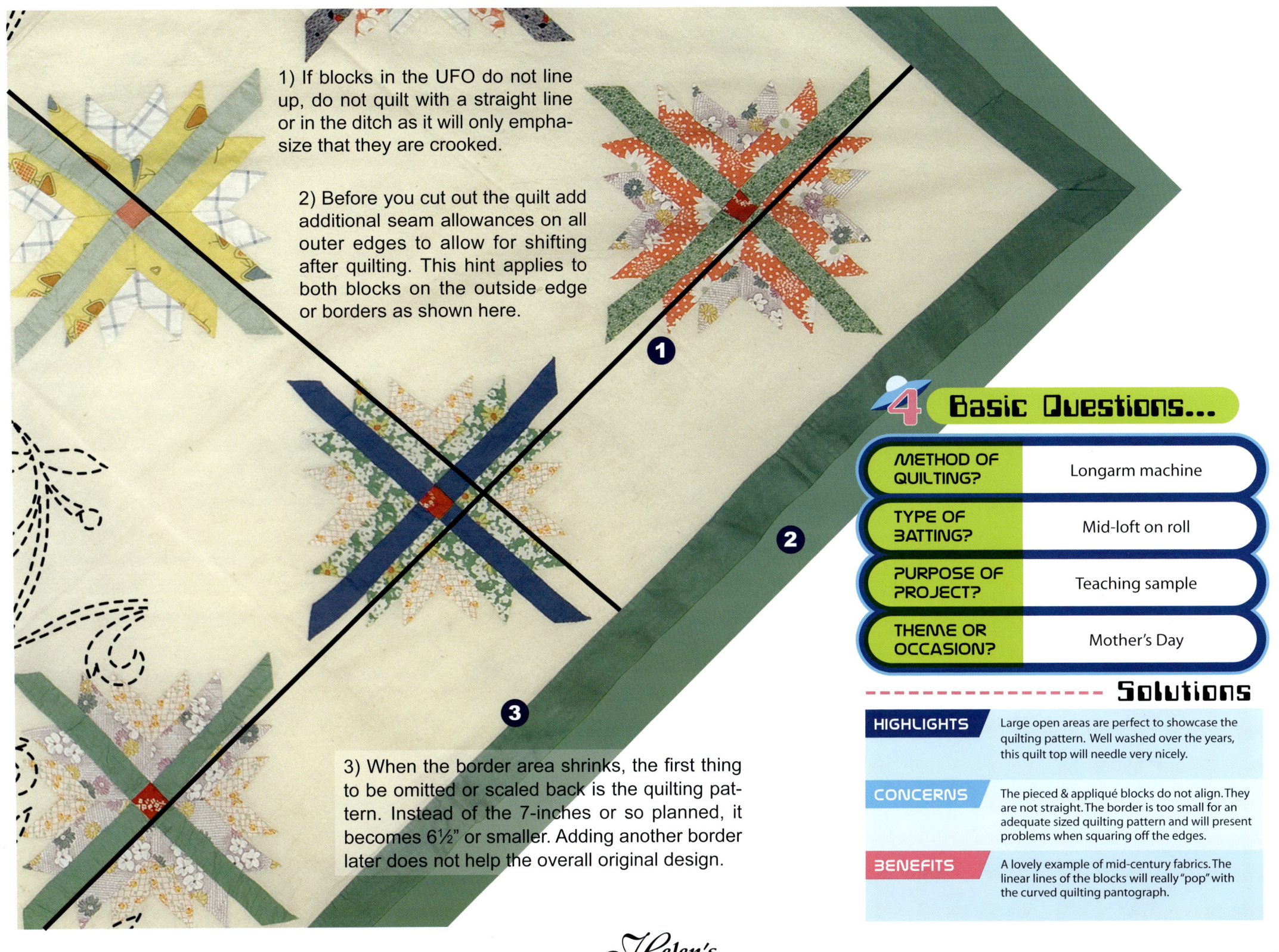

1) If blocks in the UFO do not line up, do not quilt with a straight line or in the ditch as it will only emphasize that they are crooked.

2) Before you cut out the quilt add additional seam allowances on all outer edges to allow for shifting after quilting. This hint applies to both blocks on the outside edge or borders as shown here.

3) When the border area shrinks, the first thing to be omitted or scaled back is the quilting pattern. Instead of the 7-inches or so planned, it becomes 6½" or smaller. Adding another border later does not help the overall original design.

4 Basic Questions...

METHOD OF QUILTING?	Longarm machine
TYPE OF BATTING?	Mid-loft on roll
PURPOSE OF PROJECT?	Teaching sample
THEME OR OCCASION?	Mother's Day

Solutions

HIGHLIGHTS — Large open areas are perfect to showcase the quilting pattern. Well washed over the years, this quilt top will needle very nicely.

CONCERNS — The pieced & appliqué blocks do not align. They are not straight. The border is too small for an adequate sized quilting pattern and will present problems when squaring off the edges.

BENEFITS — A lovely example of mid-century fabrics. The linear lines of the blocks will really "pop" with the curved quilting pantograph.

QUILTING UFOS with *Helen's Hints* • Helen Squire

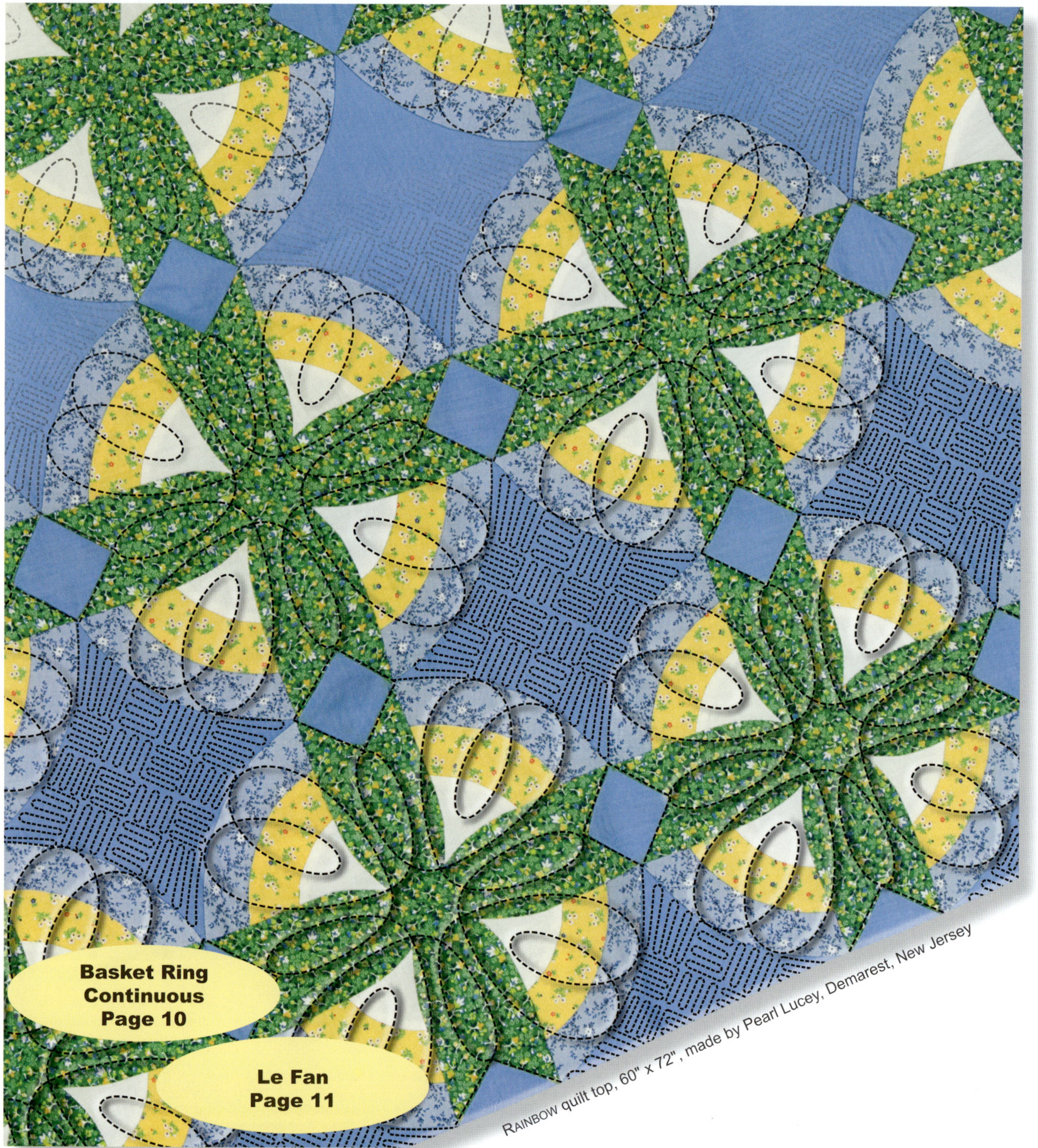

adapting patterns

Always sew a sample block before cutting out the entire quilt. Then by altering the pattern pieces before you cut out the fabric, you can avoid bulky seam allowances and create a larger area for quilting — by hand or machine. It is the first step toward pre-planning the quilting.

4 Basic Questions...

METHOD OF QUILTING?	Machine
TYPE OF BATTING?	Low to mid-loft
PURPOSE OF PROJECT?	Large bed quilt
THEME OR OCCASION?	Happy, carefree quilt

Solutions

HIGHLIGHTS — The accurate piecing makes pre-marking unnecessary when you pre-plan the quilting.

CONCERNS — By eliminating some seams from the original pattern, it is more difficult to piece.

BENEFITS — Without extra seams underneath the open areas, it takes larger patterns, is easier to quilt, and really adds to the overall effect.

Basket Ring Continuous Page 10

Le Fan Page 11

RAINBOW quilt top, 60" x 72", made by Pearl Lucey, Demarest, New Jersey

QUILTING UFOS with Helen's HINTS • Helen Squire

pressing

Some guidelines for pressing seams are: 1) press to one side; 2) press to the darker color(s) to avoid shadowing; 3) press with the bias, and towards the circular shape; 4) press to raise up the design ready for quilting; and, most importantly for this quilt, 5) press to eliminate bulk at the intersections. Use open seams when joining fabric lengths in borders and for intersections with multiple layers.

pattern making

Eliminate bulky seams entirely by redrafting the patterns, wherever possible. Instead of following the original one-fourth pattern, redraft the quarter pieces into halves and the halves into full units. These are the template pieces used in Pearl Lucey's RAINBOW quilt top.

This is not a beginner's project. It entails set-in seams and some clipping when piecing, but it is worth the extra effort to eliminate the four seams, thereby providing an open space between the circles for quilting.

markless quilting

A popular class I teach has students bringing in their UFOs – "Unfinished Objects" – for quilting suggestions. Thirty years ago Pearl would have hand quilted her hand-pieced quilt top, marking with stencils and a pencil. Today, I would suggest using a quilting design that is both machine quilted and entirely unmarked! The main quilting design is a freehand motif (see page 11). It can be stitched to the rim of the concentric circles at an imaginable clock face of 12, 3, 6, and 9 and then between those spots using the colored rings as a visual reference for height.

A variety of fillers can be quilted to add texture and dimension. Try a wave, basic stipple, flames, fan-maze, spirals, meandering, pebbles, or a basket weave (see page 10). Keep in mind that the flatter the background, the more the rainbow circle will advance and stand out.

An inherent problem with this block is the shifting and distortion of seams, caused when the pieces are sewn and pressed.

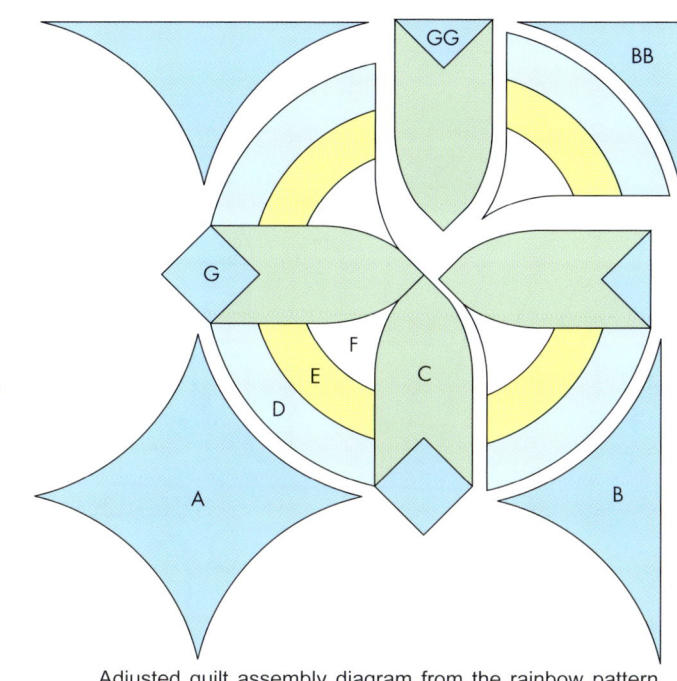

Adjusted quilt assembly diagram from the rainbow pattern collection #5050, circa 1935 by Alice Brooks.

By redrafting this pattern and omitting seams, new areas suitable for filler quilting are formed, such as BASKET RING WEAVE CONTINUOUS on page 10.

QUILTING UFOS with *Helen's Hints* • Helen Squire

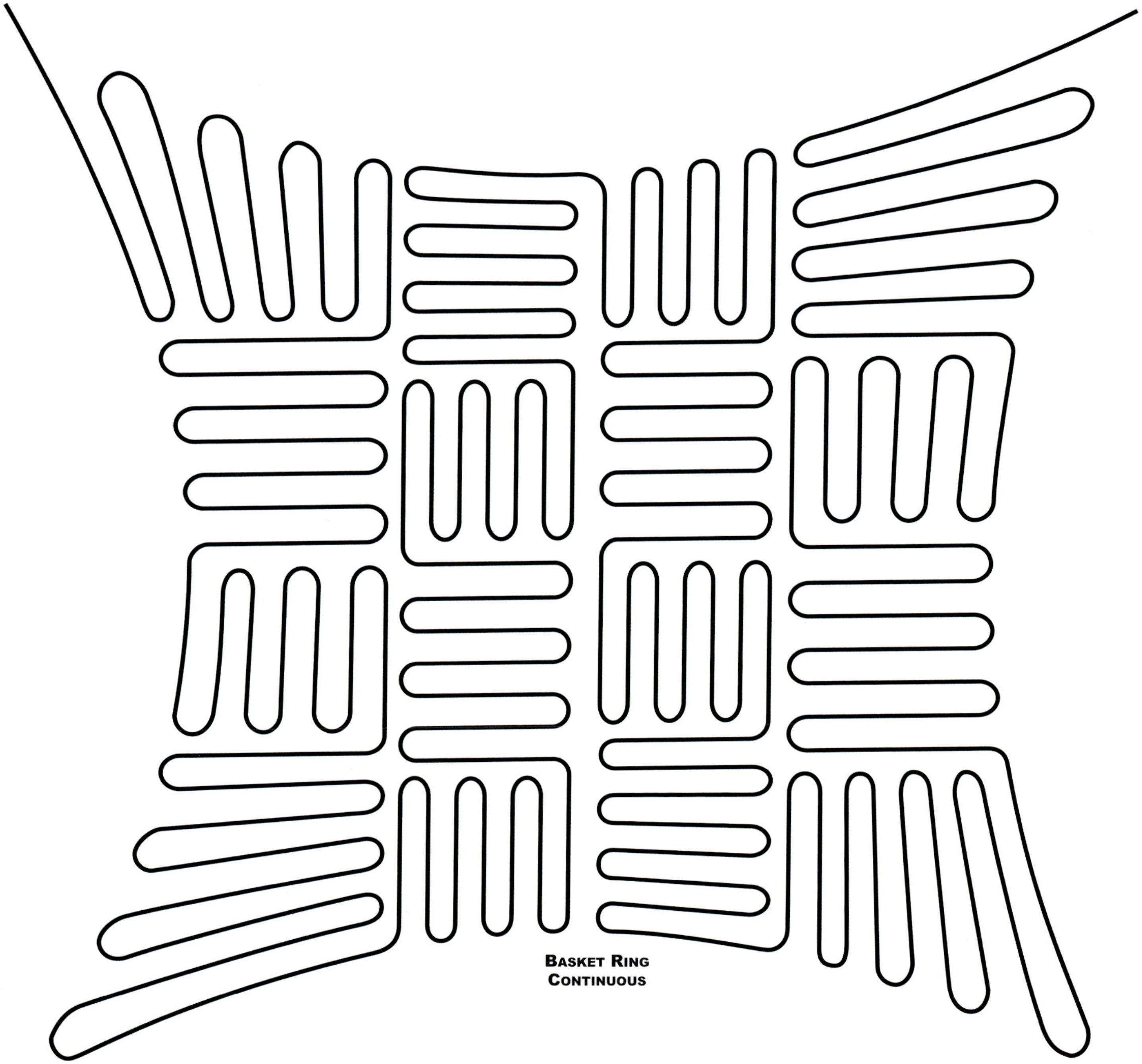

**BASKET RING
CONTINUOUS**

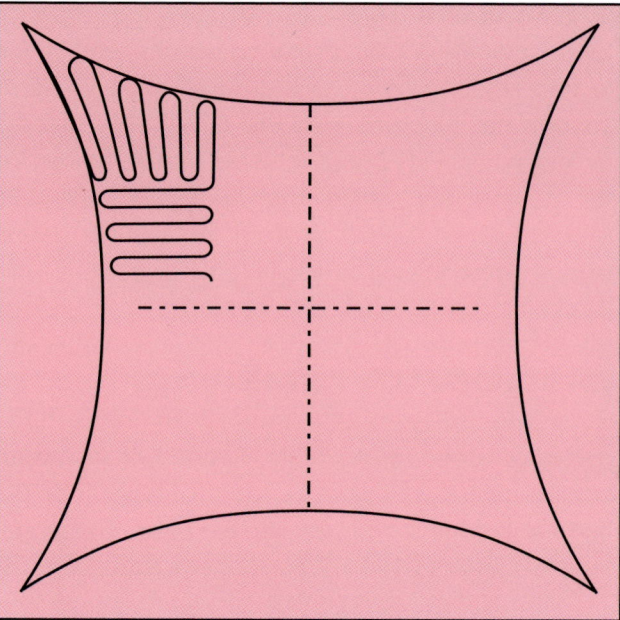

Fill the open area with freehand stitches, touching the Double Wedding Ring crescent, but not quilting in the ditch, as it would fight with the design.

The straight lines of the basket weave give contrast and emphasis to the pattern and round shape.

The most common mistake in quilting is using a pattern that is too small for the area to be quilted. Above it is placed a quarter-inch away from underneath seams. Below it is too small for the area, causing it to "float."

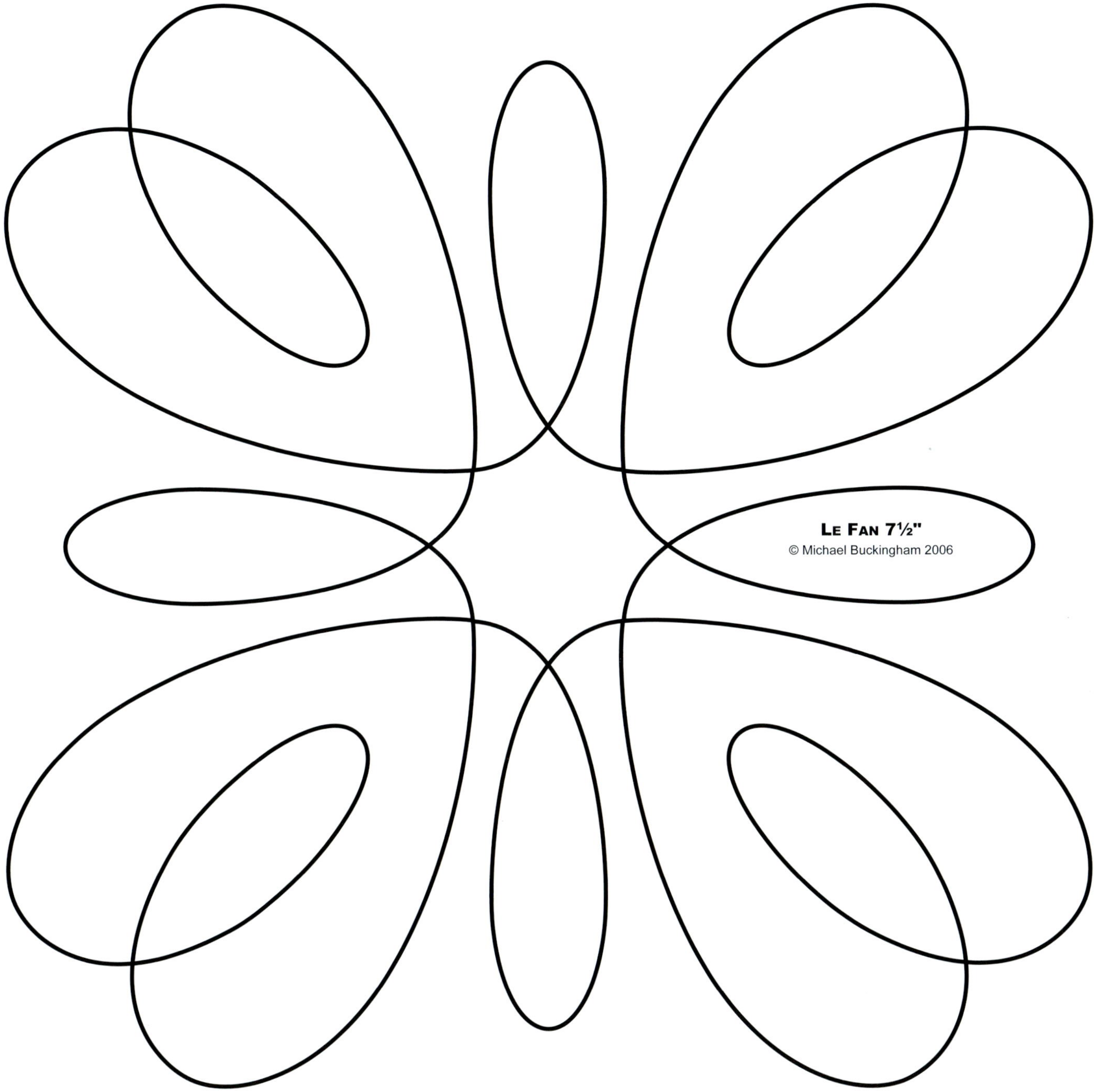

Le Fan 7½"
© Michael Buckingham 2006

QUILTING UFOS with *Helen's Hints* • Helen Squire

design choices

When choosing a quilting design for your unfinished top, you usually consider whether it will be hand or machine quilted, the type of batting you prefer, the function of the quilt—wall or bed—and the theme. The answer to these four questions will guide you to the final quilting solution.

4 Basic Questions...

METHOD OF QUILTING?	Domestic sewing machine
TYPE OF BATTING?	Low-loft poly-blend
PURPOSE OF PROJECT?	Queen-size bed quilt
THEME OR OCCASION?	Wedding gift for nephew

Solutions

HIGHLIGHTS — A large open area between the patches allows for a curved Double Wedding Ring variation, providing movement around the straight lines.

CONCERNS — The underneath seams of the patchwork pieces would be very difficult to quilt over if hand quilted. A straight edge ruler or guide is needed.

BENEFITS — Very little marking is necessary if you follow a schematic drawing and a pre-measured grid.

Cindy's Continuous Lines Page 13

Quilt top made by Cindy Dietrich, Veneta, Oregon, from a pattern by Sheila Sinclair Synder. Published by Better Homes & Gardens, American Patchwork & Quilting, April 2006.

QUILTING UFOS with *Helen's Hints* • Helen Squire

quilting area

The most important consideration when identifying each area to be quilted is choosing an appropriately-sized quilting motif. The most common mistake is choosing a design that is too small, causing a "floating effect." Since sewn seams may distort the overall measurements, choosing a quilting pattern that is flexible allows for "the fudge factor" of stretching or shortening the design.

suggestions

Two design rules came instantly to mind when I first saw this quilt top: Fabric colors that are pieced together should be quilted together, and geometric patchwork should be combined with flowing quilting. Why? It will please the eye and enhance the piecing. My suggestion to Cindy Dietrich was to quilt the faux shape of a Double Wedding Ring (DWR) design. The centric curves give overall movement to the quilt, and the pattern is especially appropriate since it was to be a wedding present for a favorite nephew!

freehand fillers

I asked talented Karen McTavish to add her McTavishing background for the open area between the rings. No pattern is necessary to create a freehand background; simply refer to a drawing.

The McTavishing technique is explained in Karen's books. Visit Kmctavish@designerquilts.com. Its free-formed swirls add movement to the geometric patchwork top.

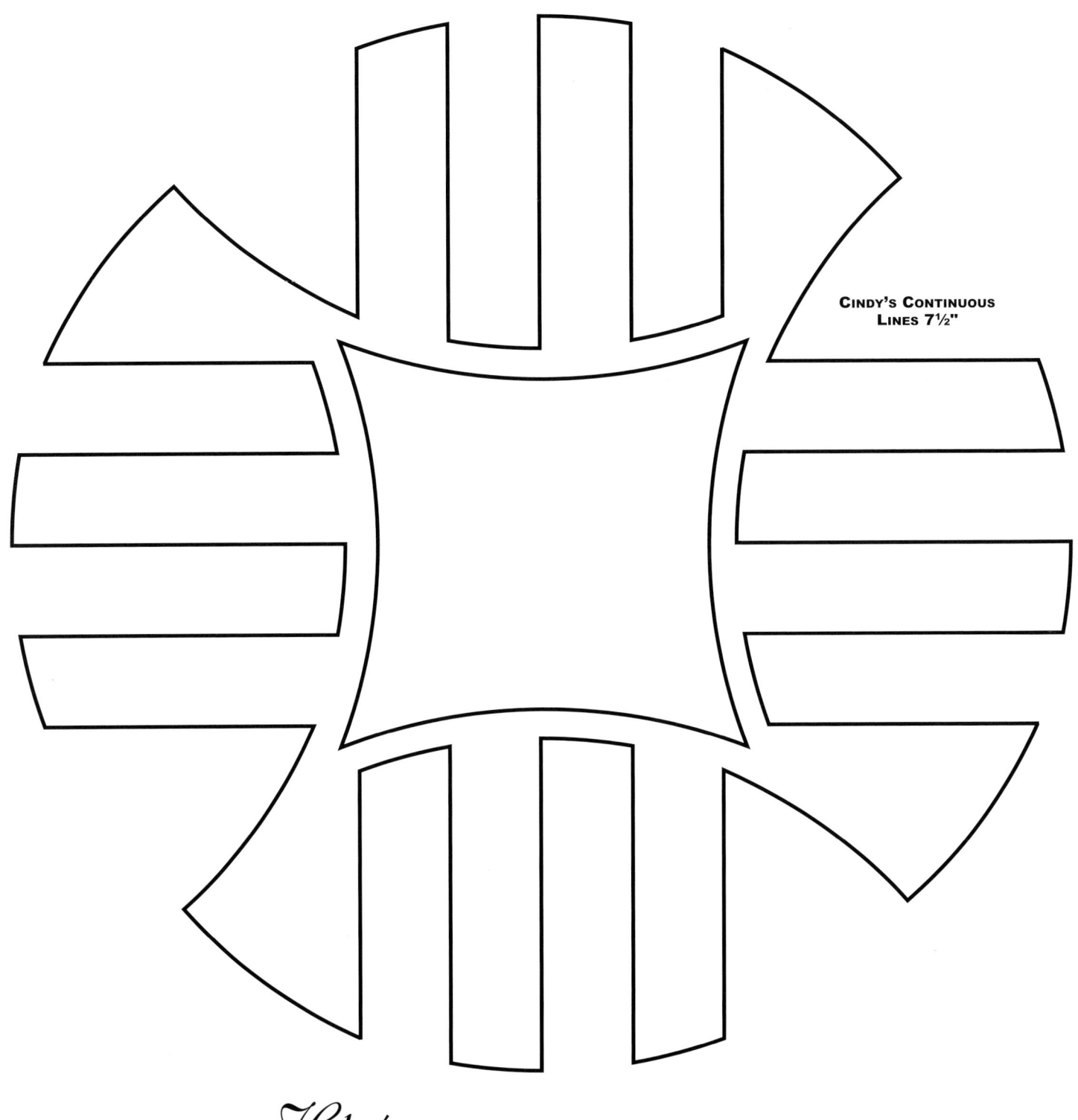

CINDY'S CONTINUOUS LINES 7½"

QUILTING UFOS with Helen's Hints • Helen Squire

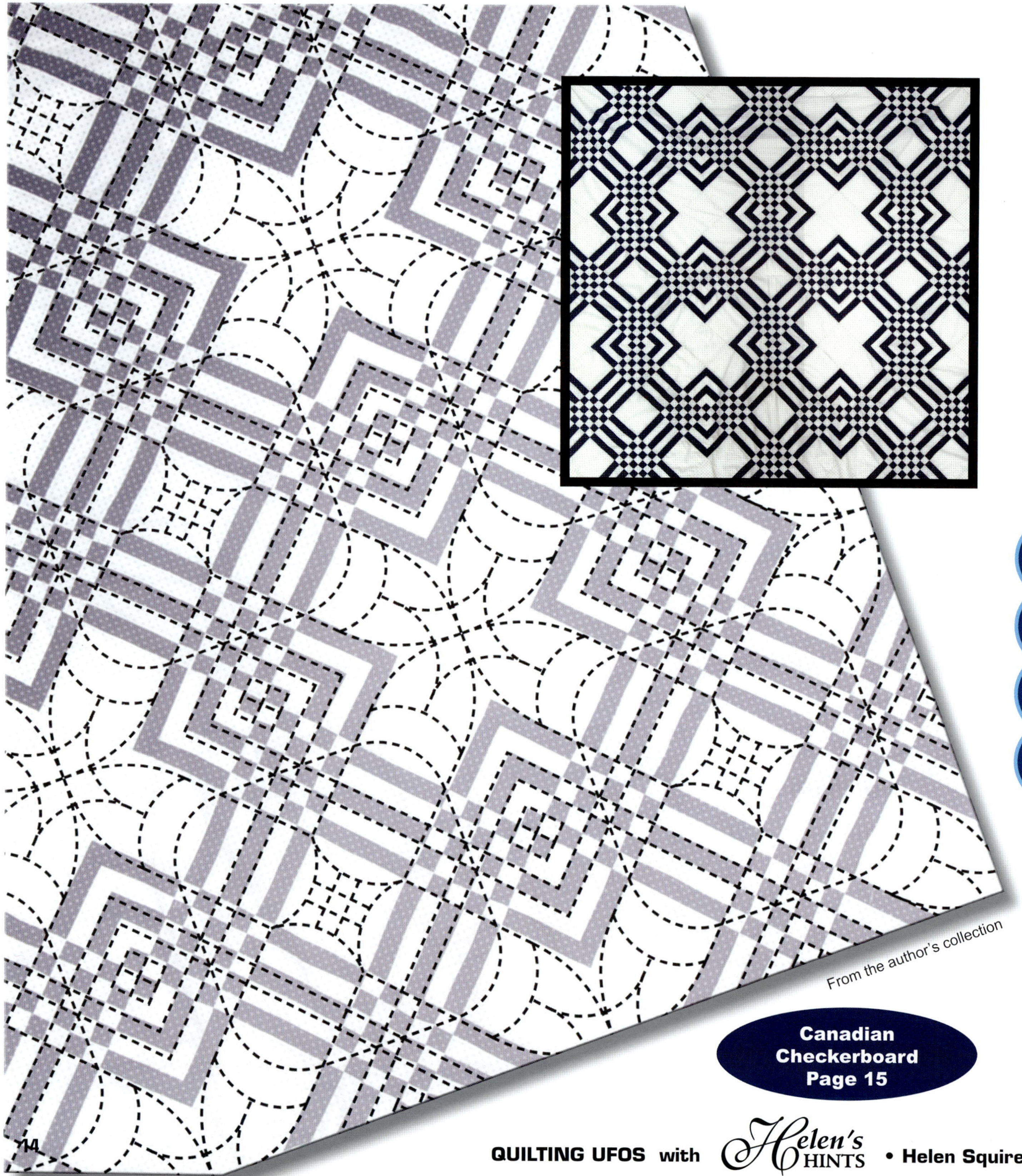

quilting principles

The rule of design is straight lines need curves, and curved lines look better next to straight lines. Think of an Amish Bar quilt with flowing feathers and a Rose of Sharon appliqué with crosshatched background lines. Combining both elements pleases the eye of the beholder.

From the author's collection

Canadian Checkerboard Page 15

4 Basic Questions...

METHOD OF QUILTING?	Longarm machine
TYPE OF BATTING?	Polyester on roll
PURPOSE OF PROJECT?	Retail sales
THEME OR OCCASION?	Masculine design

Solutions

HIGHLIGHTS — Precise machine piecing of the checkerboard and stripe patchwork provide accurate lines to outline the quilt.

CONCERNS — This is a big quilt with a large open area for quilting. Too many underneath seams!

BENEFITS — The light, white fabric permits placing the pattern underneath and using a light source to mark the design. The straight lines are easy to quilt without marking the top.

QUILTING UFOS with  • Helen Squire

strong graphics

Two separate blocks were combined in an alternating pattern using navy and white printed fabrics. It is a strongly graphic, pieced quilt pattern that calls for an equally strong, bold quilting design. The geometric and linear lines require some curves to add flowing movement. Their addition results in an oversized, secondary design that really "pops" the quilting! Their lines repeat the basic elements of the quilt top without adding fussy details.

quilting

Not every rectangular strip or 1¼" checkerboard square needs to be quilted in the ditch. By skipping rows, as illustrated, less quilting is needed and more fullness is provided especially if using a mid-loft batting. Also, try machine quilting in a soft, undulating curved stitch. It will eliminate worries about how underneath seams are pressed.

marking

Very little marking is necessary when you have a detailed sketch (schematic) to follow. The pattern CANADIAN CHECKERBOARD is perfect for filling the large open areas. Assorted background fillers can be added for extra texture.

sizes

To standardize sizes, most patterns throughout this book are presented 7–7½ inches. They can then be reduced or enlarged as needed for your project. You have my written permission.

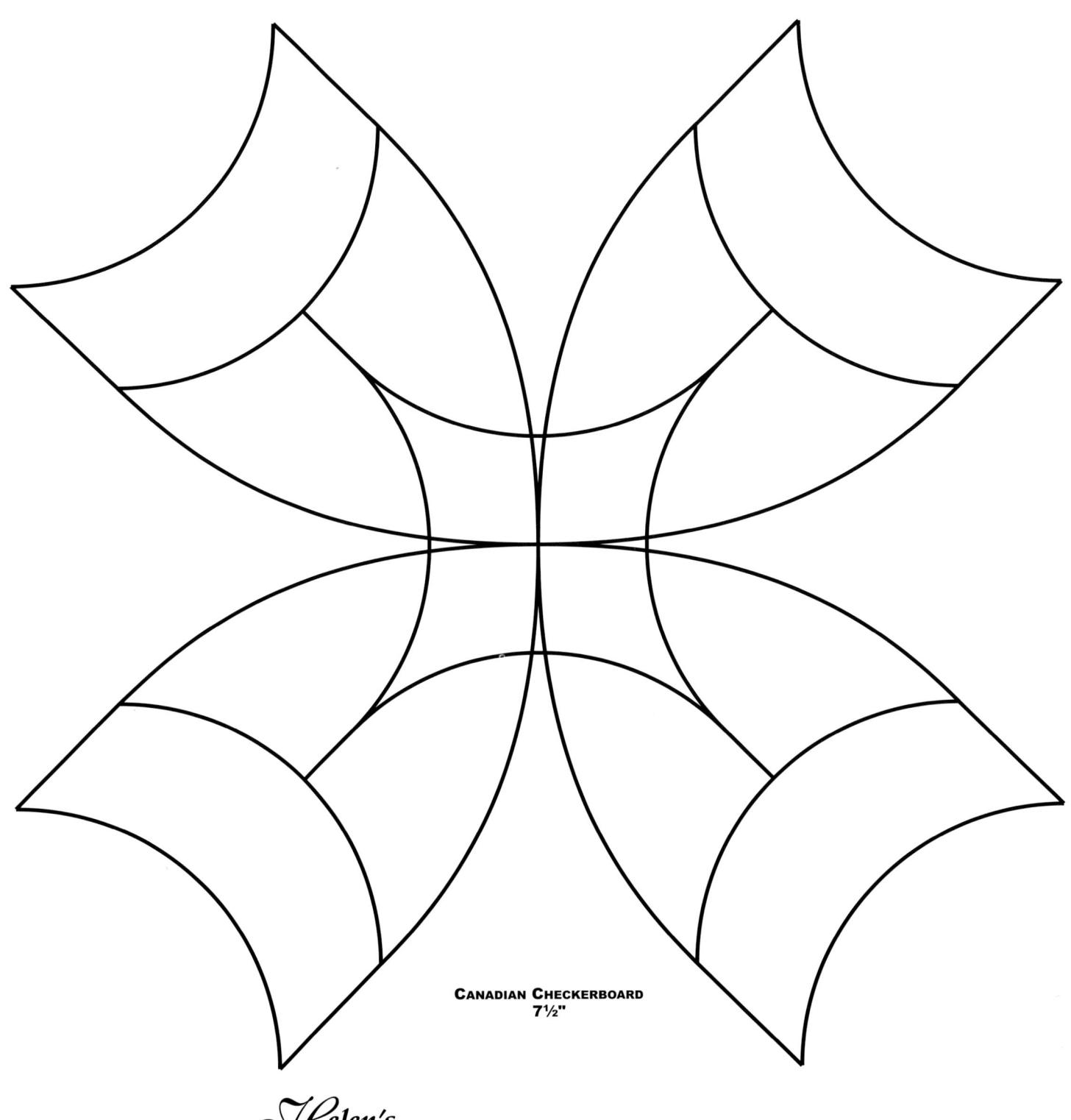

CANADIAN CHECKERBOARD 7½"

QUILTING UFOS with *Helen's Hints* • Helen Squire

vintage quilts

Antique quilt tops have unique concerns as the old fibers might have disintegrated with age and handling. Quilting large patterns using simple marking methods will help extend the life of the fabrics. The strong straight line of the blocks calls for curved lines in the quilting.

Updated Fans Page 20

From the author's collection

4 Basic Questions...

METHOD OF QUILTING?	Hand quilting or longarm
TYPE OF BATTING?	Mid- to high- loft
PURPOSE OF PROJECT?	Home decor
THEME OR OCCASION?	Family heirloom

Solutions

HIGHLIGHTS	Wonderful selection of antique fabrics from the 1800s.
CONCERNS	Life expectancy of old fabrics. Brown dyes and pigments. Very fragile blocks do not align — avoid quilting in the ditches.
BENEFITS	Large, full patterns are easier to quilt. Varying the design while keeping a common element gives additional interest. Less stitches equal less handling and stress on the fabric seams.

do not wash

This 1880s' era quilt top will probably disintegrate if washed inappropriately. "Cleanliness is not next to godliness" in quiltmaking. If you wash something very old—whether quilted or unquilted—it may literally fall apart at the seams. To preserve a family heirloom for sentimental value, only quilt it for decorative purposes and showing off in your home, not for heavy, utilitarian wear.

batting

There are dozens of different types of batting—too numerous to mention here—available for quilting. The trick to selecting the right one for each quilting project is reading the suggested basic requirement chart for how much space can be left unquilted (i.e., six square inches). For this antique quilt top, I suggested a mid- to high-loft batting. This means less quilting and allows for a larger, more simple quilting pattern.

fan pattern

The simplest way to quilt is using a fan pattern. An authentic, old-fashioned method of quilting, it needs minimum marking—usually a string with pre-measured knots, or cardboard curves to trace around in chalk—while providing structural support in an overall design.

fancy designs

That wide open block in printed stripes is the perfect place to showcase a curvaceous quilting pattern. Keep it simple and "fat," with larger block designs. Both Turkish Square, seen here, and Awesome Square, page 19, are appropriate.

Turkish Square
7½" Block

QUILTING UFOS with Helen's Hints • Helen Squire

AWESOME DELIGHT set square with extra details

TURKISH SQUARE set square

TURKISH SQUARE set on-point

For added interest use alternate rows of two patterns or more, both set square with half blocks along the edges.

QUILTING UFOS with *Helen's Hints* • Helen Squire

Corner, border, and center placement of Awesome, pg. 64

QUILTING UFOS with *Helen's Hints* • Helen Squire

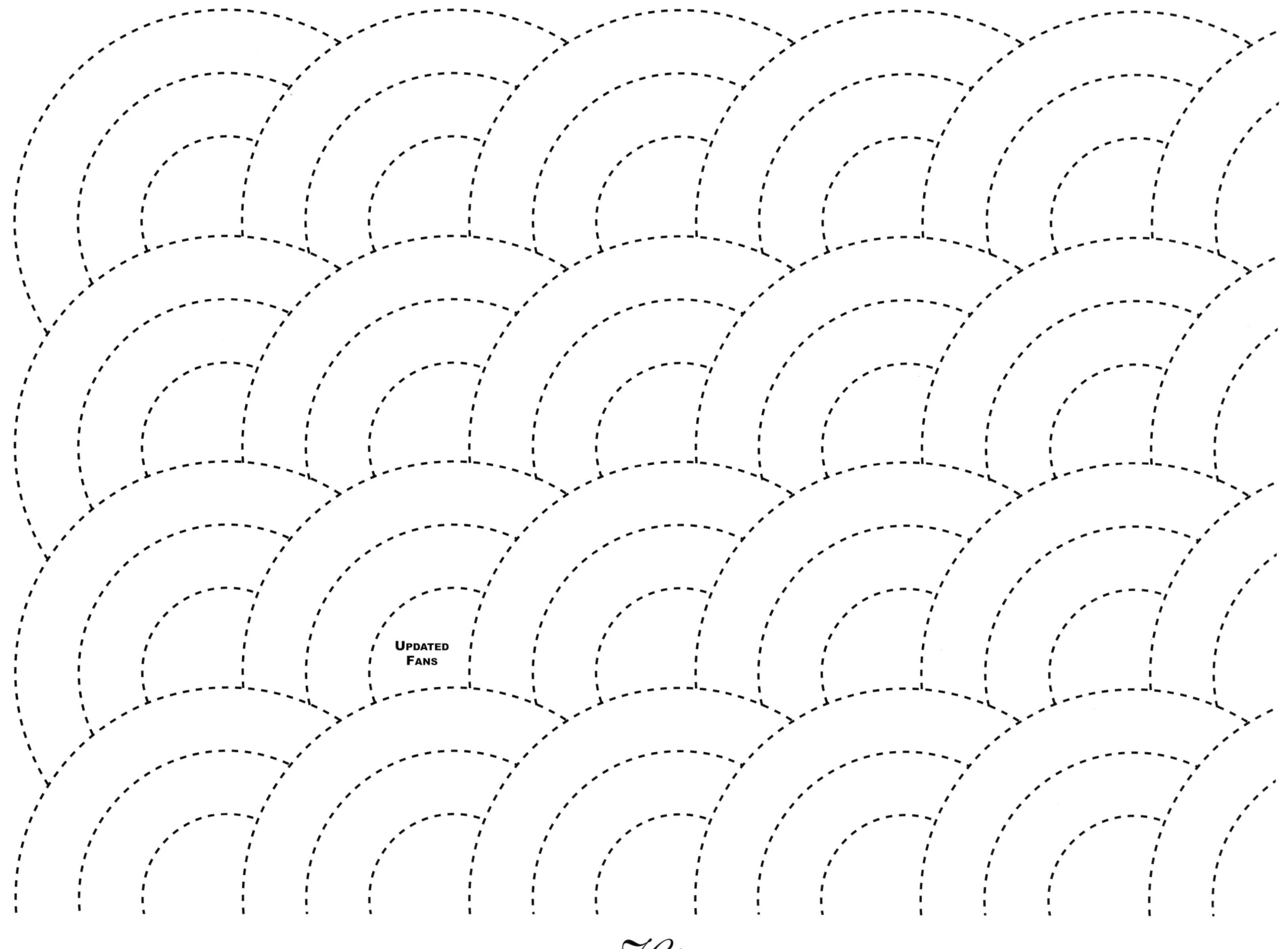

½" Diagonal Lines

Awesome Delight 7½"

marking techniques

The Odd Fellows Cross quilt had that essential "wow appeal" for a fundraising event. The problem was that the quilt top was made in the 1880s. Marking this quilt top took every trick and technique I had tried over 35 years of quiltmaking, including a silhouette stencil.

4 Basic Questions...

METHOD OF QUILTING?	Longarm machine
TYPE OF BATTING?	High-loft polyester
PURPOSE OF PROJECT?	Fundraising raffle
THEME OR OCCASION?	Nutcracker Suite Ballet

Solutions

HIGHLIGHTS — Bold, holiday colors and wide open areas for quilting make this a spectacular quilt. Has a great wow factor.

CONCERNS — The tri-color antique fabrics would require very different marking tools. The quilt measurements from top to bottom edge vary by 6 inches.

BENEFITS — Professionally marked and quilted by quilters who can "hide the mistakes" and work in the fullness. Thank you, Janie Donaldson.

When asked by the The National Quilt Museum in Paducah to provide a raffle quilt. I knew I had just the right quilt top in my collection. The holiday colors and crisp patchwork—with its wide open areas—were perfect for a great looking quilting pattern. As seen in American Quilter magazine, Winter, 2005.

Kaylee's Square Page 23

Kaylee's Border Page 25

QUILTING UFOS with Helen's Hints • Helen Squire

marking tools

KAYLEE'S SQUARE is a very forgiving pattern when you mark the scrolls and swirls. It can be shortened or lengthened to fit any odd-sized blocks as long as the points are placed uniformly ¼" away from the triangles and off the seams underneath.

The quilting lines for the four-block, half-square triangles are drawn with an acrylic ruler. Create a square with triangles that are the same size as the patchwork block. Each pair will match even though not perfectly "squared off." These quilted triangles form a continuous straight line between the rows. They reinforce the idea of diagonal lines framing the quilting motif and effectively minimize the background area in the corners.

other suggestions

I prepared a pantograph pattern with multiple repeats taped together for one length of the quilt. Unfortunately, the pantograph was then deemed unusable because of the wavy sides of the borders. The triple borders surrounding the blocks were not straight. They had been pulled, stretched, and eased together, resulting in ruffles that do not measure the same on both sides of the quilt. The quilting pattern in the entire border had to be adjusted and traced using the light box technique.

fabric concerns

Different colored marking devices were necessary because of the non-colorfast dyes used in the vintage fabrics. A white chalk pencil was used on the red and green fabrics, and a pink chalk pencil on the white fabric. The popular pounce technique, using a slotted stencil with powder brushed over the design, or white or grey powder sprayed from an aerosol can, would not work on this tri-colored quilt top.

7" KAYLEE'S SQUARE

One-quarter of the quilting design

Extra sewing seam allowance

pre-plan marking

I plan one quarter of the quilting design and an extra few inches for the repeat on muslin or paper. 1) Copy the block pattern onto cardboard, and cut the outline to use as a silhouette stencil. 2) Position multiple repeats of the border to fit the perimeter, and identify the corner miter and the center of the top. 3) Slide the paper pattern under light fabric and use a light source to trace wherever possible.

reversed pattern

To miter any corner, you need three copies of the pattern—one of which should be a reverse. If you rotate the pattern you will not use it, but a reversed copy gives you more possibilities.

This border's miter is a mirror image of the design.

KAYLEE'S BORDER 2"

KAYLEE'S BORDER 3"

QUILTING UFOS with *Helen's Hints* • Helen Squire

structural quilting

Because it's to be quilted by hand, the quilting lines can stop and start by scooting into the batting—to create a second hexagon in the center—echoing the seams of the six-pointed star, a very geometric shape. A classic cable design quilted around the border adds movement.

From the author's collection

Kentucky Star
Page 27

Rickey Cable Border
Page 30

4 Basic Questions...

METHOD OF QUILTING?	Hand
TYPE OF BATTING?	Mid-loft
PURPOSE OF PROJECT?	Twin bed quilt
THEME OR OCCASION?	Grandma made it.

Solutions

HIGHLIGHTS	Good hand piecing with nice color placement. A wide border will showcase the hand quilting.
CONCERNS	The 1930s' printed fabric has already determined the scale and proportion suitable for quilting. Needs a small, dainty, flowing design or cable to add interest.
BENEFITS	Following the seams with outline quilting or quilting in the ditch means very little marking is required.

QUILTING UFOS with Helen's Hints • Helen Squire

fudge factor

My biggest peeve with borders is that teachers—myself included—did not tell you years ago, when those UFOs were made, to add extra seam allowances along the outside edges of the quilt in order to have a fudge factor when the quilt shifts during quilting. We all cut out batting larger than the quilt top, then cut around the batting by 2–4 inches for the backing. The poor quilt top only has ¼" seams included!

extra seam allowance

I recommend adding a 2" seam allowance instead of ¼" on all pieces that touch the outside edges. When you cannot square off the quilt, the first thing you start to eliminate is the area for quilting. You cut back on the size of the pattern, hoping that will make a difference.

Adding extra seam allowances (except when it's a foundation or paper-pieced border) will give you the fudge factor, with more room to finish your pre-planned quilting design, square off the four corners, and to sew on the bias binding or finishing trim.

shifting

This is the ah-ha moment in my workshops. Everyone seems to relate to the same problem of the quilt top "shifting" after quilting.

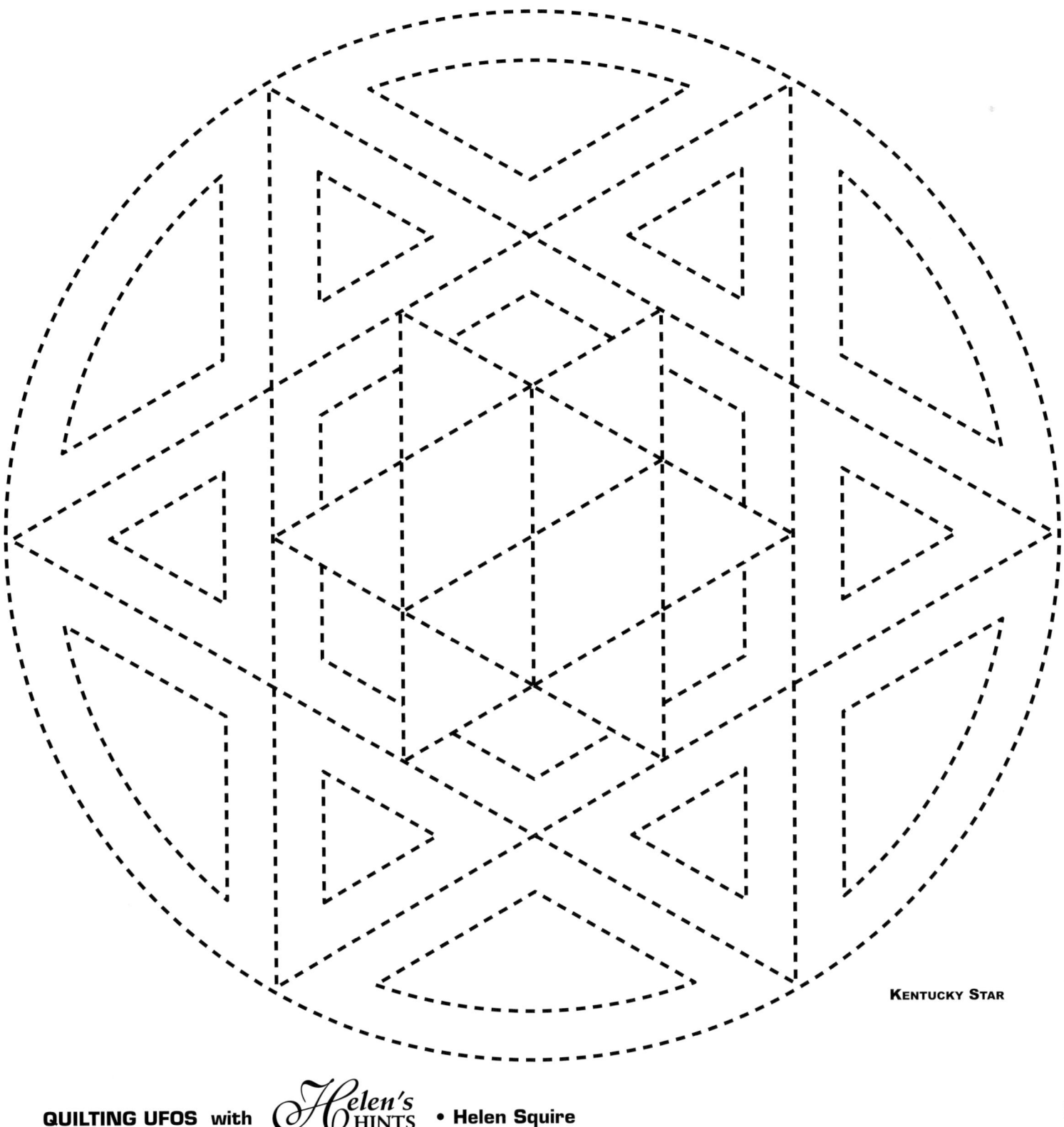

KENTUCKY STAR

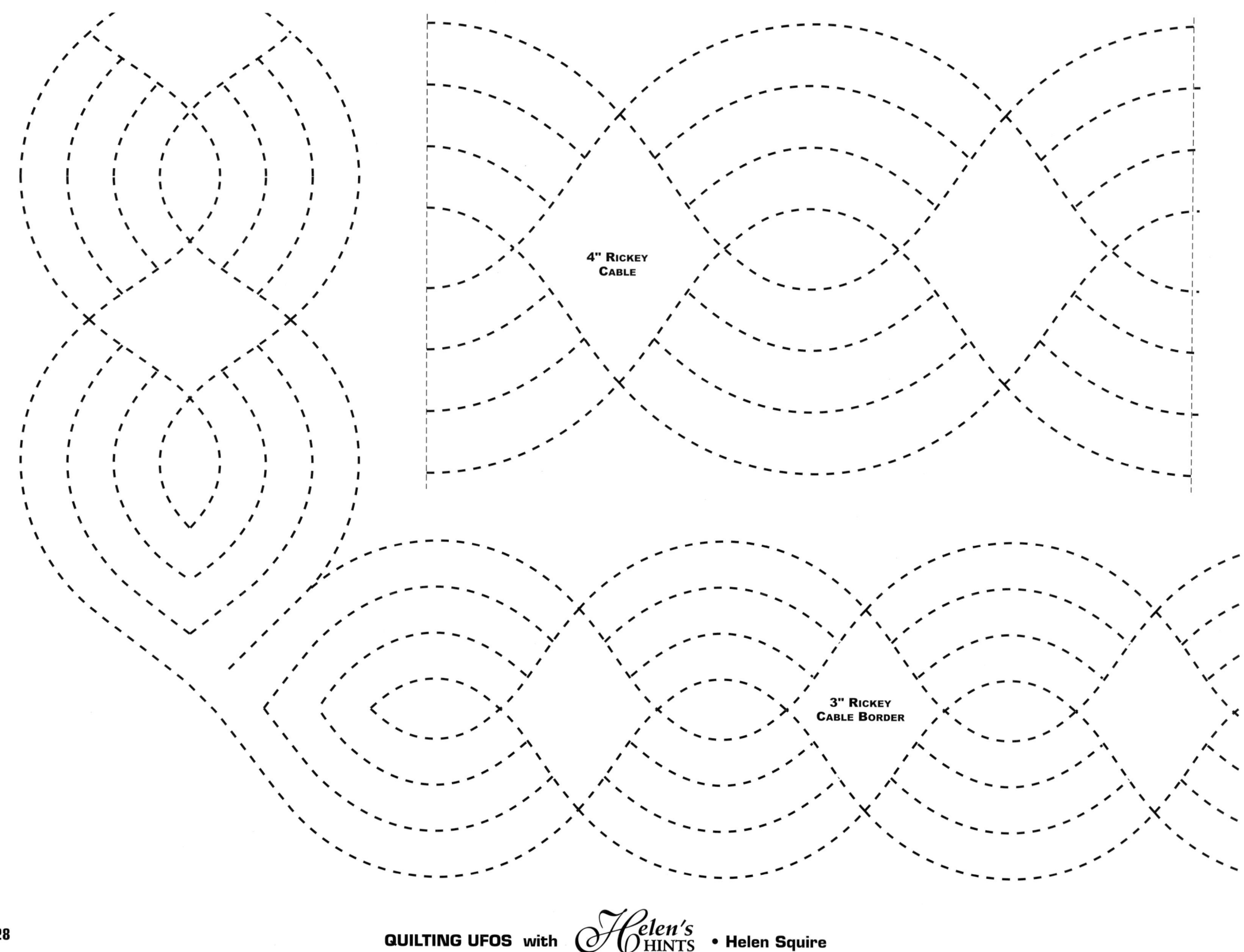

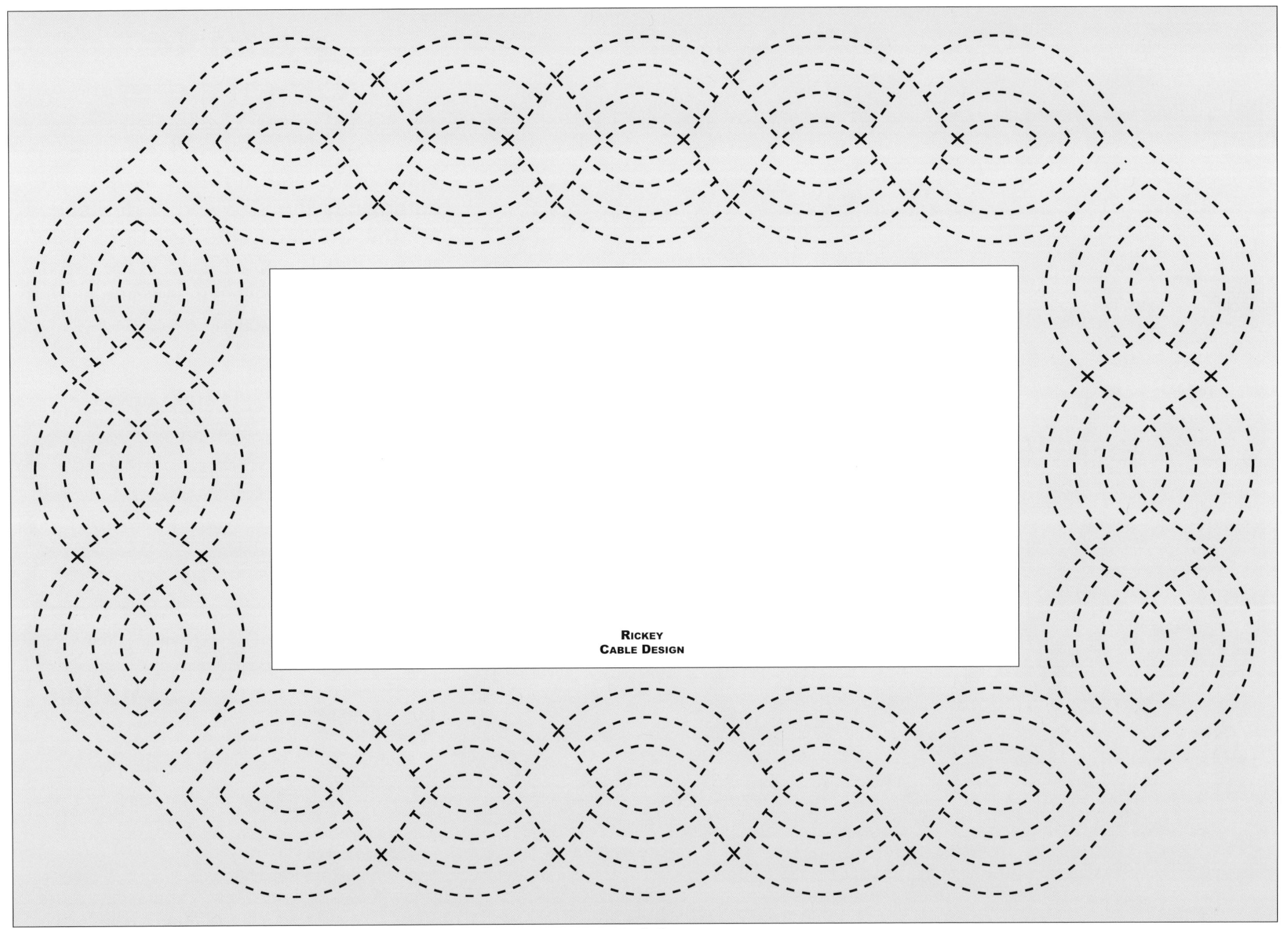

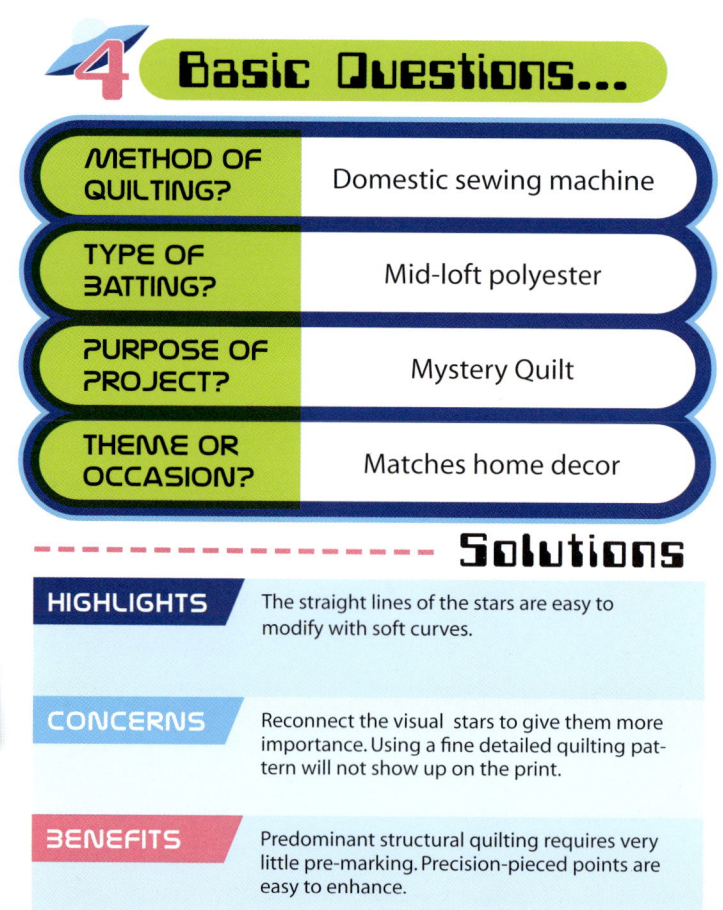

The Tool Box quilt top, 66" x 81", made by Candace Casciano, Newington, Connecticut, a member of the Greater Hartford Quilt Guild. This was a mystery quilt project. Pattern by Beth Ferrier, Applewood Farm Publications, www.applewd.com/patterns/page19.html.

fabric choices

The fabric you selected and used in making the quilt top has already pre-determined the size and scale needed for the quilting patterns. Here small quilting details would be lost in the overall, wildflower print, while the precision piecing makes structural quilting a breeze.

4 Basic Questions...

METHOD OF QUILTING?	Domestic sewing machine
TYPE OF BATTING?	Mid-loft polyester
PURPOSE OF PROJECT?	Mystery Quilt
THEME OR OCCASION?	Matches home decor

Solutions

HIGHLIGHTS — The straight lines of the stars are easy to modify with soft curves.

CONCERNS — Reconnect the visual stars to give them more importance. Using a fine detailed quilting pattern will not show up on the print.

BENEFITS — Predominant structural quilting requires very little pre-marking. Precision-pieced points are easy to enhance.

fabric selection

Those wild, exciting prints or that tiny, busy folk art fabric—hunted for and collected years ago—can come back and haunt us when we finally decide to quilt. It has predetermined the scale and size of the quilting patterns.

Remember when you learned how to make a sampler quilt and the teacher told you to select a large, medium, and small printed fabric and two coordinated solid colors? Well, that would have been the perfect time to think about the quilting!

mystery quilt

When Candy Casciano was told by the Newington Schoolhouse Quilters to bring fabrics for the Mystery Quilt challenge, she had no clue what the final quilt would look like. Had she known, another focus fabric—again considering scale and size—would have been selected.

modified outline

My immediate UFO suggestion was to highlight the larger, predominate star shapes with slightly curved lines. This creates a secondary design—circles around the smaller stars—that provides structural quilting and emphasizes the precise piecing of the triangles.

area to be quilted

Once the basic outline is planned, it becomes apparent that the busy print prevents using an elaborate quilting pattern along the borders and in the parallelogram shape, as it will not be seen.

The shape is large and needs something else. The question is what? As a designer, I do not always know what is right but I can feel what is wrong. Candy and I are still on a quest to find the appropriate pattern.

CANDACE

VIRGINIA REEL LEFT

VIRGINIA REEL RIGHT

QUILTING UFOS with *Helen's Hints* • Helen Squire

planning the quilting

There are three places to plan the layout of the quilting design:

1) at the corners facing inward;
2) at the centers of the quilt, facing out toward the edges; and
3) midway between, as in swag designs.

Any pattern can be made to miter at the corners and reverse at the centers. You need three copies of the pattern, one of them a reverse.

Another possibility is to flip or flop the pattern—illustrated below—so as to nestle the shapes closer together, thereby minimizing the background area.

Center reverse   Flip and nestle   Miter and reverse

VIRGINIA'S CORNER 1

VIRGINIA'S CORNER 2

QUILTING UFOS with *Helen's Hints* • Helen Squire

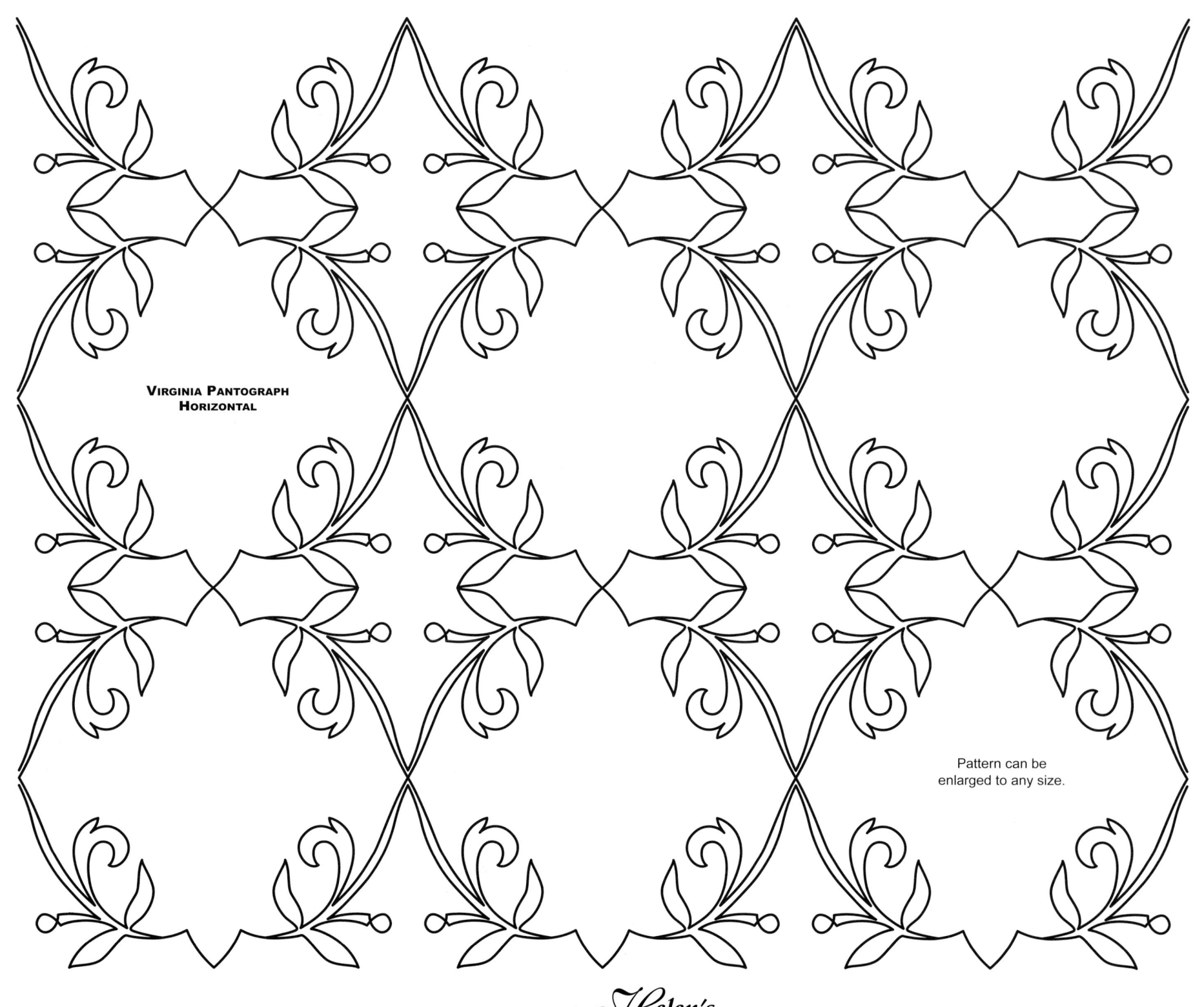

HEARTS AND FLOWERS BORDER

corner possibilities

There are no limits to possibilities when planning corners. Shown here are only three: 1) Daisy flowers face into the quilt and miter into four on stems. 2) The rosette of hearts is predominately placed and small details are eliminated at the miter. 3) Daisy flowers face outward and miter into three in the corner. Make extra copies of the one you like best. It does not need to be reversed as they are already mirrored images.

❶ ❷ ❸

QUILTING UFOS with Helen's Hints • Helen Squire

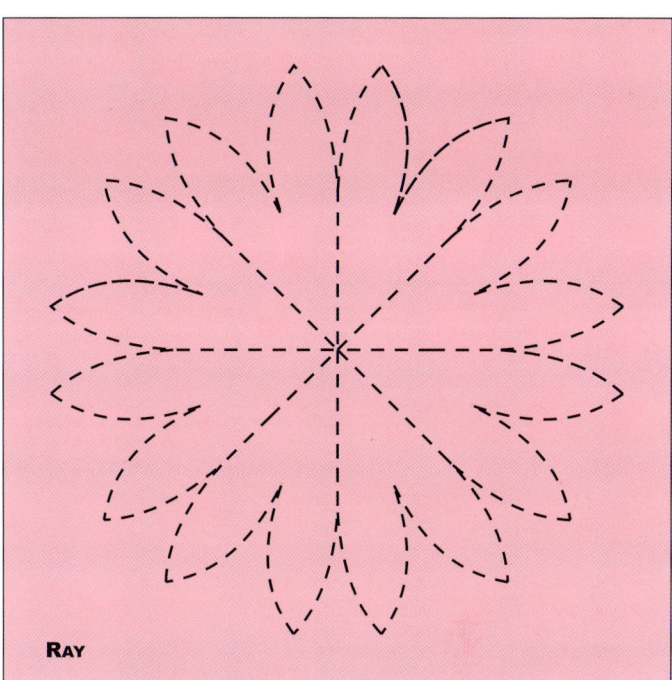

RAY

These two smaller patters are formed by selecting or omitting details from the original. They can now be enlarged to any size.

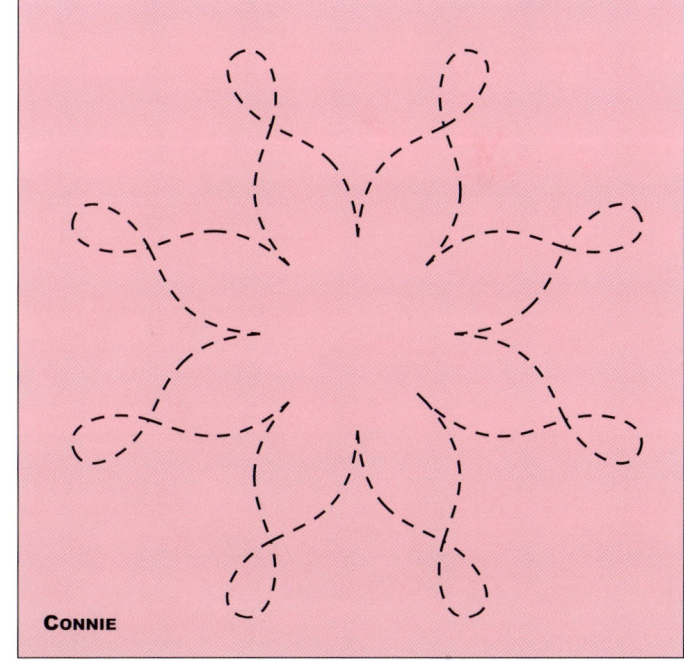

CONNIE

RADIANCE
7" CONTINUOUS

southwestern quilt top

It was serendipitous to have an appliqué UFO quilt top in class, as most are usually already quilted. It was important to find a simplified—yet strong—graphic that set off the blocks without competing with the variety of inner borders. A modified version of the quilt is shown here.

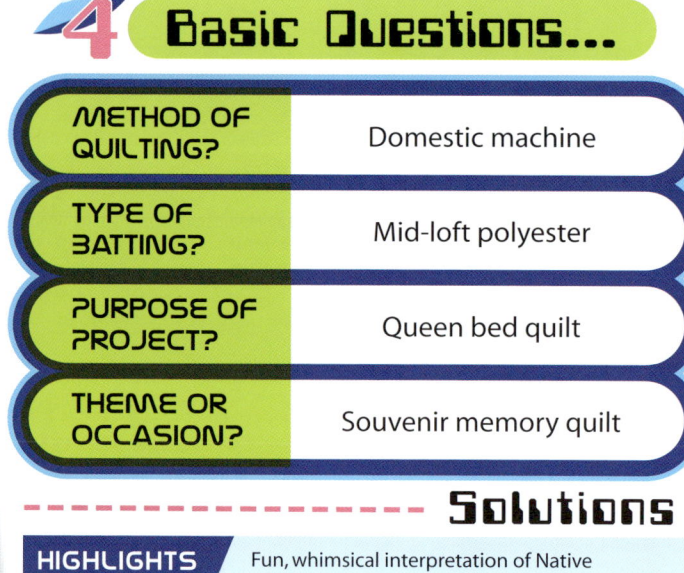

4 Basic Questions...

METHOD OF QUILTING?	Domestic machine
TYPE OF BATTING?	Mid-loft polyester
PURPOSE OF PROJECT?	Queen bed quilt
THEME OR OCCASION?	Souvenir memory quilt

Solutions

HIGHLIGHTS	Fun, whimsical interpretation of Native American icons and symbolism
CONCERNS	Most underneath seams are pressed open preventing quilting in the ditch. The 25 different types of borders around the block area present a challenge. (See page 42)
BENEFITS	Good, equal distant placement of the pieced and appliquéd blocks makes planning and marking the sashing and outer border easier.

Computer modified version of SOUTHWESTERN quilt by Rosemary Hopkins, St. Louis, Missouri

Warrior Shield Page 42

QUILTING UFOS with *Helen's Hints* • Helen Squire

Back view of pressed seams

appliqué decision

Use two rows of stitches, the first a close outline, and the second a quarter-inch away to add importance. This is called echo, contour, or ripple quilting. The open and pressed seams in the borders prevent quilting in the ditch.

QUILTING UFOS with  • Helen Squire

Back view of pressed seams

outline quilting

Quilt as close to the appliqué as possible to raise up the design. Not every detail needs quilting, just enough to lock in the fullness and identify the motifs. Quilting around the diamonds in the border will showcase their shape.

QUILTING UFOS with *Helen's Hints* • Helen Squire

background texture

Additional birds can be quilted in the sky, while a horizontal line delineates the ground behind the figure. Outline quilt on one side only of the narrow appliquéd stems, as quilting both sides would make it too flat, and it's really not needed.

QUILTING UFOS with *Helen's Hints* • Helen Squire

Pattern can be enlarged to any size.

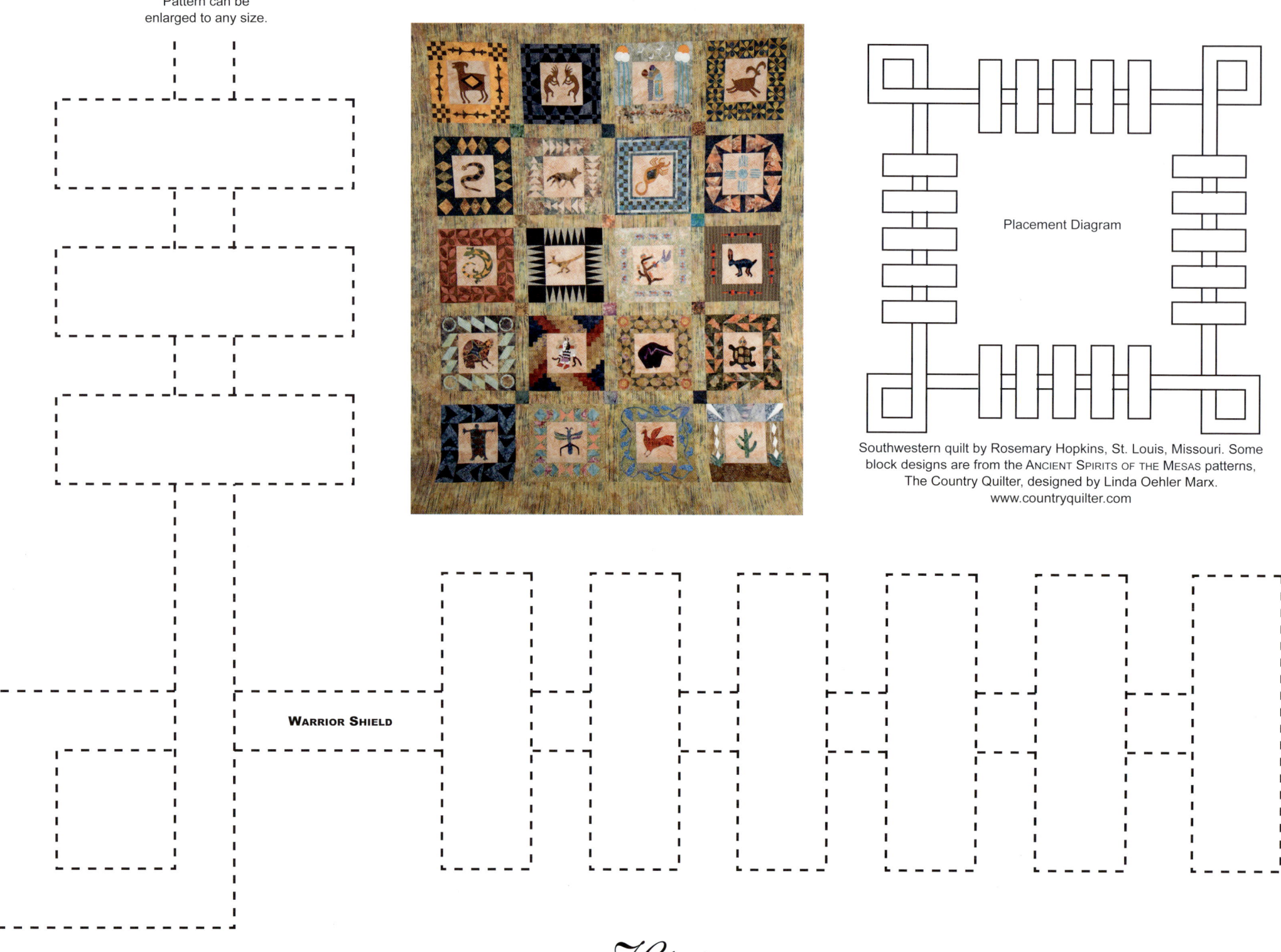

Placement Diagram

Southwestern quilt by Rosemary Hopkins, St. Louis, Missouri. Some block designs are from the ANCIENT SPIRITS OF THE MESAS patterns, The Country Quilter, designed by Linda Oehler Marx.
www.countryquilter.com

WARRIOR SHIELD

QUILTING UFOS with *Helen's Hints* • Helen Squire

Celestial Variation 4½"

double miter

One of the many variations possible in the Celestial Cable series is using a double width reversed, with mitering at the corner and extra stitches inside the diamonds. When folding the pattern to miter the corners, correction fluid is used to eliminate smaller details.

Glorified Chain 2"

QUILTING UFOS with *Helen's Hints* • Helen Squire

embroidery inspired

A linen tablecloth—with its lovely blue flowers—was the inspiration for two completely different series of quilting patterns! The embroidered details, shown above and on page 32, so intrigued me that I spent a full Mother's Day playing around with design variations. The VIRGINIA REEL and VALERIE patterns are the result.

This timeless floral motif, VALERIE, was designed specifically to have an echo row of stitches—similar to the quilting used in Hawaiian applique. This ripple, contour quilting style, when placed around the entire motif, lends a greater presence and importance to the overall design, and keeps it separate from the background.

VALERIE
8" x 7½"

simplify, simplify

Look for the essence of the basic shape—what makes it special—and work with that image. Eliminate smaller details, enlarge parts of the design, and trace and re-trace on paper until you like the results. Then make multiple copies and start having fun!

matching blocks

Once a corner is designed four copies are needed to plan a companion block. Draw a square and place an image at each corner. Next determine if they should touch or be kept separate with a connecting bridge. This is very important when planning a rectangular quilting pattern.

placement

A pattern will look different when placed square or on-point. Refer to the illustration on page 18. It will also change based on the background fill. Grid lines, echo quilting, and textured fillers will also influence the overall appearance. Try different possibilities.

The biggest change is when a pattern is placed facing in or facing out. There are many good illustrations of the phenomenon throughout the book, but look ahead to page 53—the REDWORK WHIMSY blocks—for a prime example.

variations

It's hard to believe that one simple design—VALERIE—can be coaxed into a block, sashing strip, baskets, and wide multi-repeat border with grid! Turn the pages to see for yourself, and try designing your own variations.

VALERIE REVERSED
8" x 7½"

gridlines

MAUREEN 7" BLOCK

Patterns can be enlarged to any size.

Crosshatch

Curved contour

Diagonal straight lines

QUILTING UFOS with *Helen's Hints* • Helen Squire

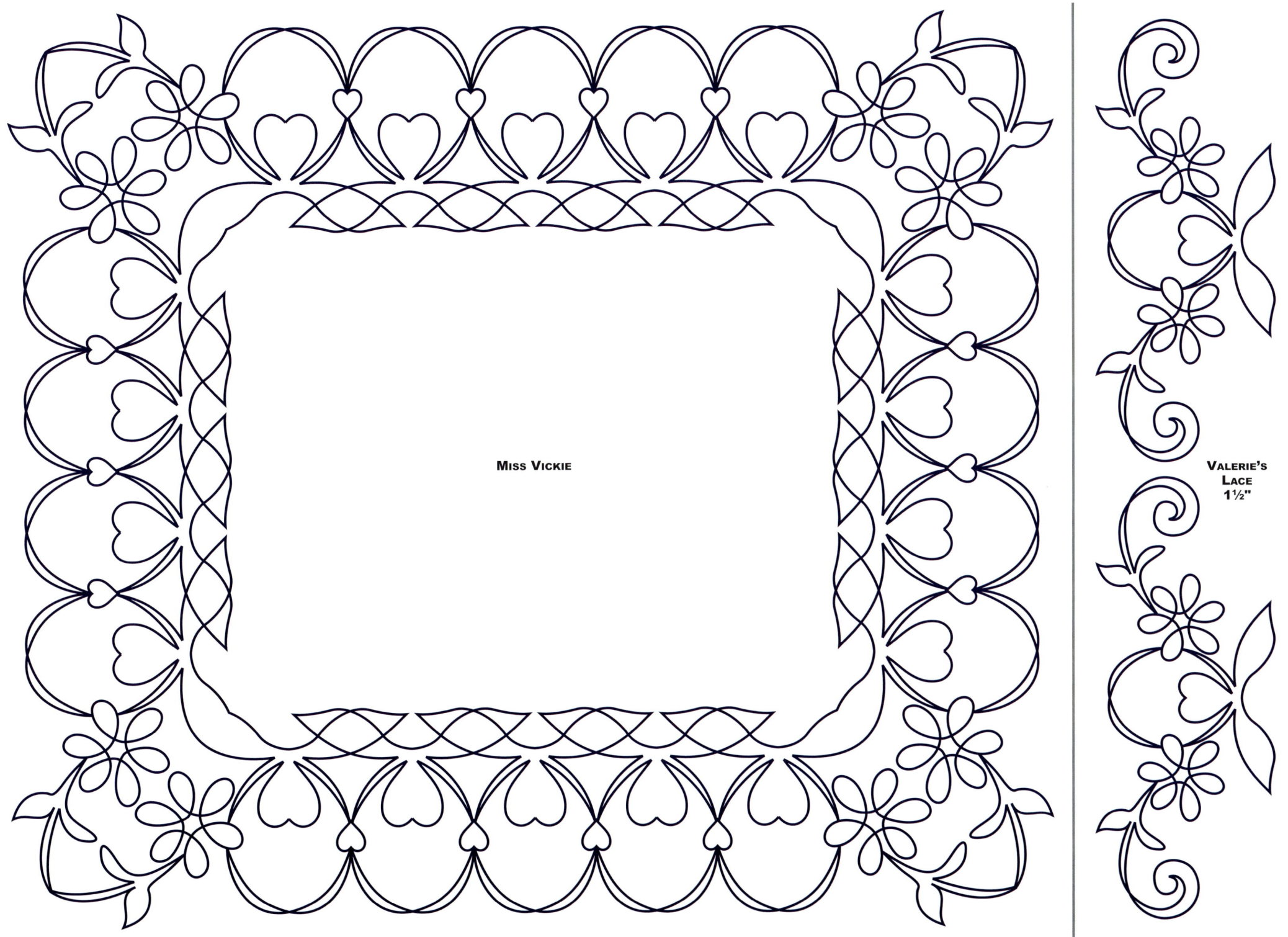

QUILTING UFOS with *Helen's Hints* • Helen Squire

VALERIE'S FLOWER BASKET
7½"

½" Crosshatch

QUILTING UFOS with *Helen's Hints* • Helen Squire

creating a border

Quilting patterns that have fluid movement are often used in place of actual applique to break up the straight lines of a grid background.

Free-motion machine quilting—or hand stitches—can both be used to quilt these graceful, very forgiving floral arrangements. Flatter background textures will raise up the design even more. Add gridlines and texture—and even use colored pencils to bring this bouquet to life!

VALERIE'S BORDER

1940s era, makers unknown

freehand embroidery

Machine quilters who recently discovered the beauty and ease of using freehand filler backgrounds can now take it to the next level and create continuous free-formed pictures! Simple key elements—leaves, scrolls, and flowers—are placed, repeated, and reversed to form a leafy bough surrounding birds sitting on a branch.

continuous-line

On closer examination, one marvels at the freedom of the original artist's style. Her seemingly effortless way of connecting the shapes give movement and a whole new perspective to the words "continuous-line." Imagine. This so-called modern quilting technique was drawn and sewn in redwork embroidery nearly 65 years ago!

wholecloth linens

Inspired by Cindy Needham's book *Wholecloth Linen Quilts*, I was searching for vintage linens—a pillowcase or tablecloth to quilt—and bought this lawn tea-towel specifically because its folk-art style matched my existing design, BENJAMIN, in the book *Helen's Mix & Match Quilting Patterns*. Cindy then gave me a linen cloth from her own collection with almost the same redwork embroidery images! There are similarities and differences. Both have chain-stitched machine embroidery in heavy red thread, bird and flower motifs, and are approximately the same size. The skill levels vary and are more complex in the interpreted, overall design.

origin

I have not researched the original source of these old patterns, but believe it to be some type of promotional premium. Kits of this era would have been pre-stamped and would not have allowed for this much diversity. My patterns and variation were simplified and drawn with the sewing equipment and threads of todays quiltmakers in mind.

QUILTING UFOS with *Helen's Hints* • Helen Squire

Detail of embroidered birds. How many wings are on the bird on the right? Now that is called poetic license!

EMBROIDERED BIRD

Patterns can be enlarged to any size.

Key elements of these designs are the leaves, scrolls, and flower motifs.

QUILTING UFOS with *Helen's Hints* • Helen Squire

REDWORK WHIMSY
SQUARE

pattern placement

Design facing outward

Design facing inward

QUILTING UFOS with *Helen's Hints* • Helen Squire

REDWORK WHIMSY BLOCK

Patterns can be enlarged to any size.

½" Horizontal Gridlines

WHIMSY ON-POINT

Patterns can be enlarged to any size.

½" Horizontal Gridlines

botanical plants

a quilter's garden

In 1987, I had two books published simultaneously—*Dear Helen, Can You Tell Me All About Quilting Designs?* (American Quilter's Society), and *A Quilters Garden: From Plants of the Holy Land* (Revell Publishing). To pay homage to the 20th anniversary I wanted to include the plants and some of the text. For more details and information visit the AQS Web site, www.AmericanQuilter.com.

The twelve plants included here were chosen for their symbolism and pleasing appearance. The botanical features were carefully researched for authenticity. As quilting patterns, these designs rely on your needle to paint a picture.

adding texture

They are not chubby hearts to outline the quilt, but simplified designs representing real-life plants, trees, and flowers. To make them work, they require texture and dimension, created with puffy close-ups, flat backgrounds, and smoothly flowing quilted lines.

adding color

Designs today can be embellished with colored pens and pencils, embroidery, thread painting, and with all types of applique: fusible, shadow, and traditional. Some embroidery is needed for details too small to be seen quilted.

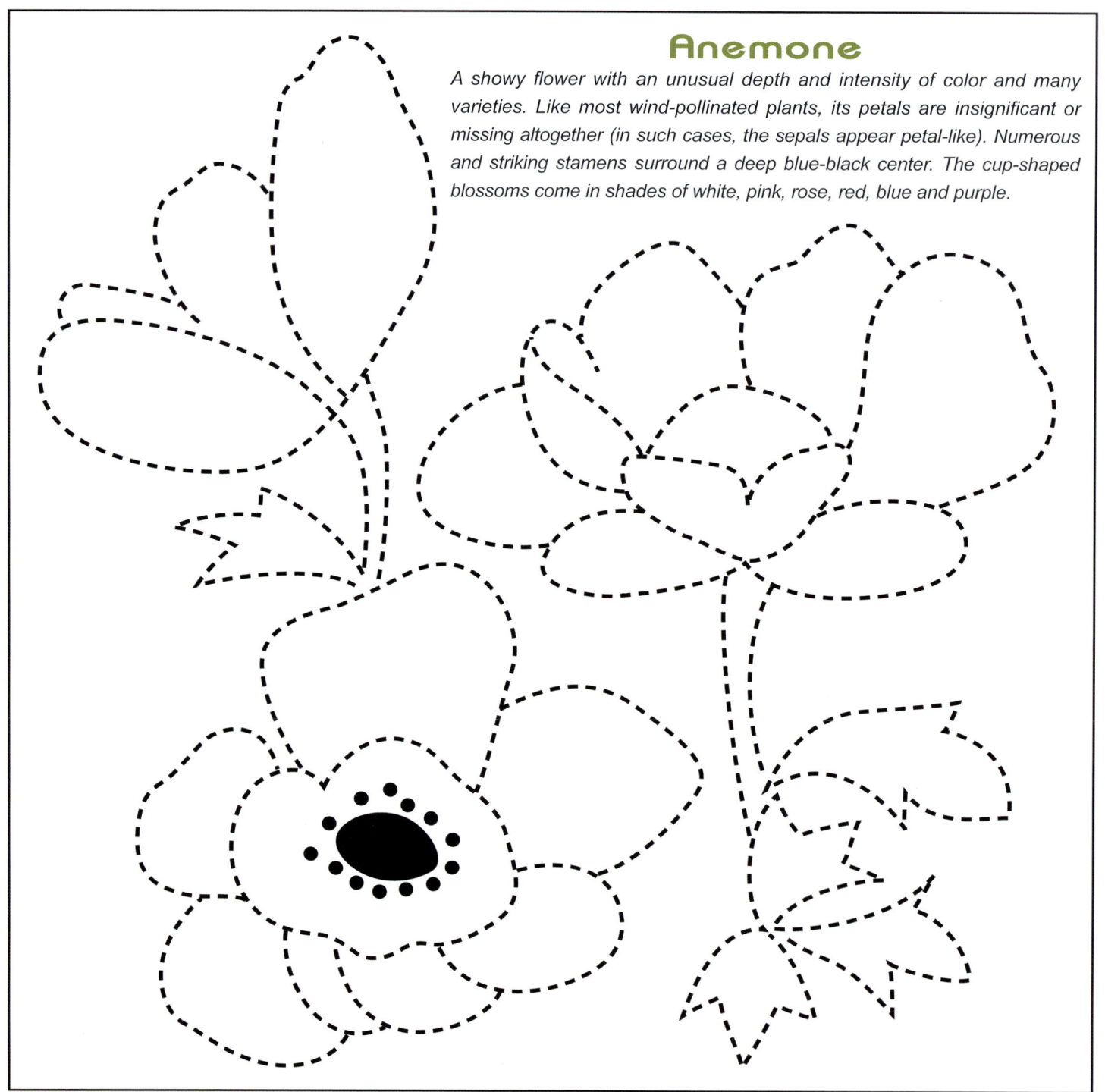

Anemone

A showy flower with an unusual depth and intensity of color and many varieties. Like most wind-pollinated plants, its petals are insignificant or missing altogether (in such cases, the sepals appear petal-like). Numerous and striking stamens surround a deep blue-black center. The cup-shaped blossoms come in shades of white, pink, rose, red, blue and purple.

QUILTING UFOS with *Helen's Hints* • Helen Squire

A decorative sewing caddy can sit over the arm rest of your favorite chair, holding sewing supplies. It is an excellent project for beginning quilters who want to try a small quilted sample before making a wallhanging or quilt. It is also a great item to make for fundraising events!

Iris

The yellow flag iris shown here is a direct descendent of the original wild species that grows from thick underground stems known as rhizomes or roots. Irises have six petal-like floral segments—the more erect inner ones (petals) are called standards while the usually drooping outer ones (sepals) are called falls.

The Greeks, impressed with their stunning range of colors, named the plant iris after the Greek goddess of the rainbow.

QUILTING UFOS with *Helen's Hints* • Helen Squire

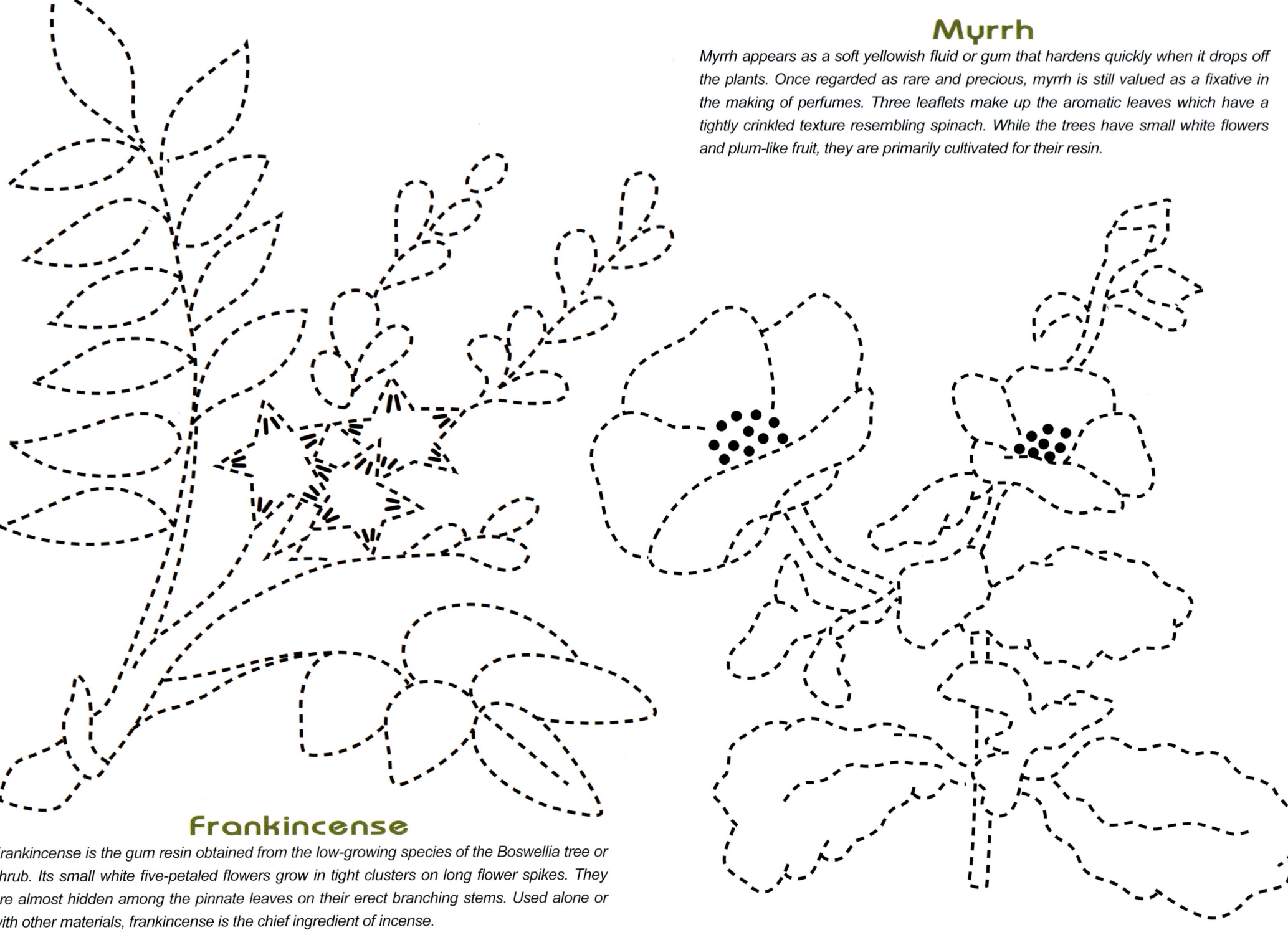

Myrrh

Myrrh appears as a soft yellowish fluid or gum that hardens quickly when it drops off the plants. Once regarded as rare and precious, myrrh is still valued as a fixative in the making of perfumes. Three leaflets make up the aromatic leaves which have a tightly crinkled texture resembling spinach. While the trees have small white flowers and plum-like fruit, they are primarily cultivated for their resin.

Frankincense

Frankincense is the gum resin obtained from the low-growing species of the Boswellia tree or shrub. Its small white five-petaled flowers grow in tight clusters on long flower spikes. They are almost hidden among the pinnate leaves on their erect branching stems. Used alone or with other materials, frankincense is the chief ingredient of incense.

QUILTING UFOS with Helen's Hints • Helen Squire

Apricot

The apricot is a good shade tree that grows 20 feet tall with a spread of 25–30 feet with dense foliage. Early spring brings a profusion of white or pink cupped blossoms with five petals, borne singly or doubly at a node, on very short stems. In summer, a golden yellow fruit appears where the flowers bloomed.

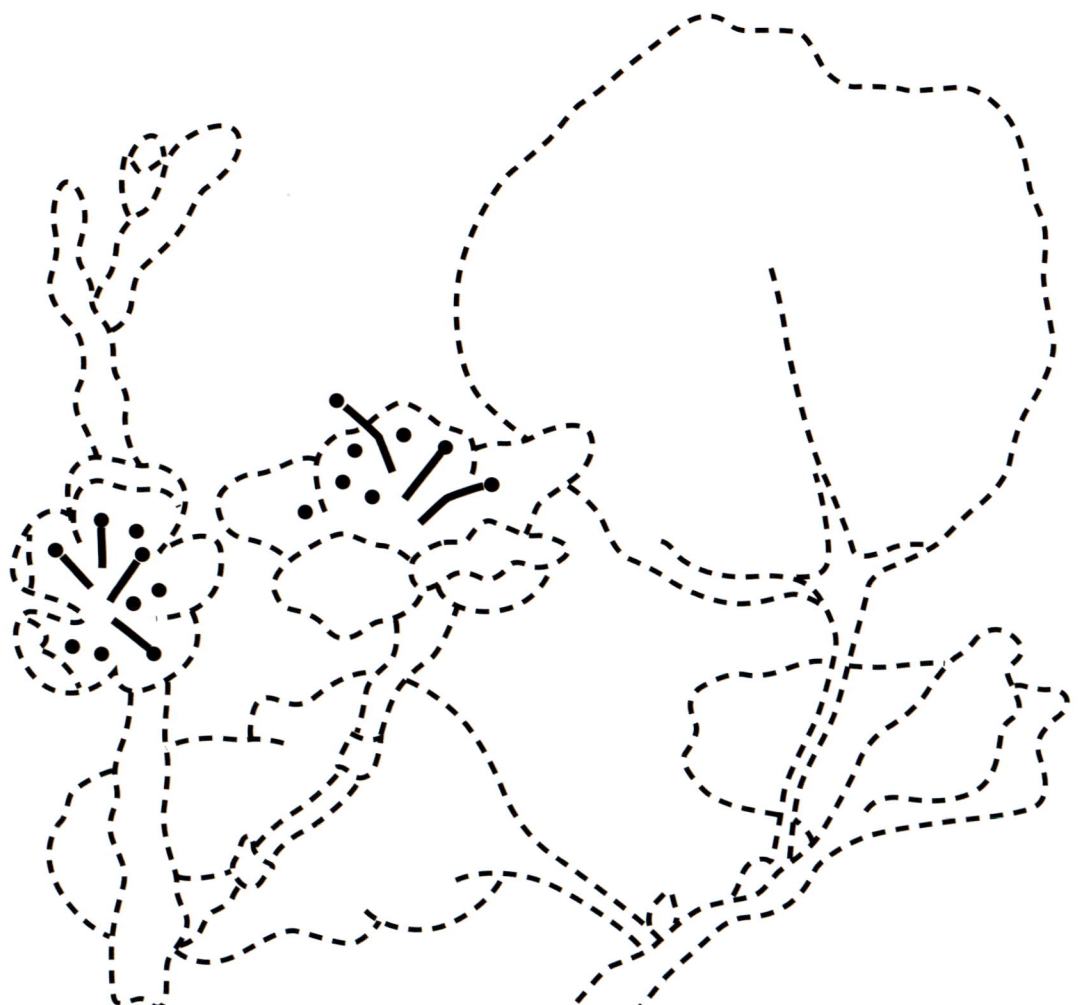

Embroidery is necessary to give authenticity. The stamen (or filament), attached at its base to the flower, has an anther for catching pollen at its free end.

Pomegranate

Pomegranate refers to both the small shrub-like tree and its fruit. It grows 12–20 feet tall, with bright green lance-shaped leaves and thorns. The bell shaped flowers are borne toward the ends of the branchlets. The fruit is a large berry—about the size of an orange, but with a smooth leathery skin. Colors range from brownish yellow to purple, or the more familiar scarlet red.

Add embroidery to give textures as the thorns are too spikey to be quilted. The petals grow crumpled in the bud so French knots give dimension to the tightly curled blossoms.

Flax

Flax flowers have five petals and are usually blue—sometimes whitish in color. Narrow leaves grow alternately on the stalk. This is a tender annual plant with small globular bolls that contain the seeds.

Flax, one of the oldest textile fibers and made into linen, has been found in ancient Egyptian tombs. Valued for its strength and durability, the smooth surface of the linen repels soil. Stronger than cotton, it dries more quickly, and is more slowly affected by exposure to sunlight.

Modern uses of flax—for twine, or rope, and flaxseeds for linseed oil and cattle fodder—were not known in biblical times. Flax fibers are also used for canvas, fire hoses and fishnets, and products that require strength and the ability to withstand moisture.

Embroidery is necessary to enhance the flax quilting design: a straight stitch for the stamen and a double overcast stitch at the tips.

Crocus

Easily recognizable, these small bulbous crocuses have grassy leaves and short stems that bear one solitary elongated flower. A low-growing herb, its cup-like flowers bloom abundantly in shades of purple, lavender, white, and yellow. The stigmas of the flowers are narrow, thread-like, and a vivid orange color.,

"Meadow Saffron," also called autumn crocus, is grown and harvested for stigmas which are picked from the centers of the flowers and dried. They can be ground, or used in whole strands or pressed cakes. It would take a field of flowers to provide enough golden saffron for spicing. Almost 4,000 stigmas are used to make one ounce of saffron.

The expensive saffron is valued for both its flavoring and coloring properties. Once used for dyeing textiles, we now know it better as a yellow vegetable dye useful to color butter, cheese, and confections. It is also used in medicine.

Use embroidery to enhance the feathery stigmas with either the satin stitch or chain stitch.

QUILTING UFOS with *Helen's Hints* • Helen Squire

Olive

The olive is a slow growing evergreen tree with a thick twisted trunk and many branches. Its leaves—leathery and lance shaped—are dark green on the top and silvery gray underneath. They grow opposite each other on the stem. The white flowers (not shown) are borne in loose clusters and have four sepals and petals. Its small fleshy oval fruit has a stony seed inside. The fruit is either harvested in the green unripe stage, or when it matures to a dark purple or black.

Fig

Fig trees can grow from 12–25 feet tall and equally as wide with large leaves and thick foliage. The inconspicuous greenish-colored flowers lack petals. Tiny figs develop at the juncture of the old wood and new buds. The "fig fruit" is actually the stem tip—a fleshy pear-like receptacle called syconium. The inner walls are the true fruit, all edible and delicately sweet. Oblong figs grow one to three inches and are mostly white, brown, or purple in color when ripe.

QUILTING UFOS with *Helen's Hints* • Helen Squire

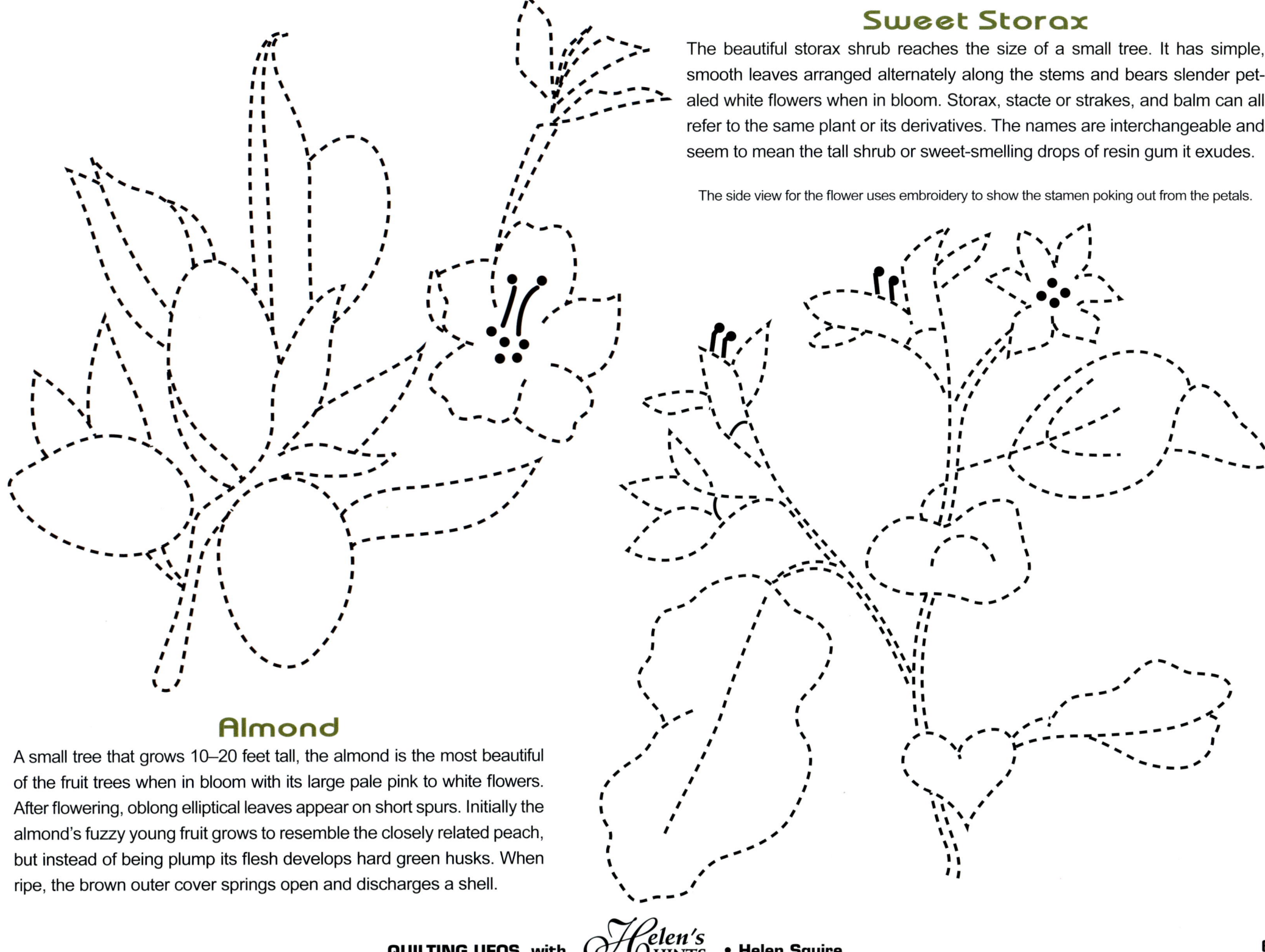

Sweet Storax

The beautiful storax shrub reaches the size of a small tree. It has simple, smooth leaves arranged alternately along the stems and bears slender petaled white flowers when in bloom. Storax, stacte or strakes, and balm can all refer to the same plant or its derivatives. The names are interchangeable and seem to mean the tall shrub or sweet-smelling drops of resin gum it exudes.

The side view for the flower uses embroidery to show the stamen poking out from the petals.

Almond

A small tree that grows 10–20 feet tall, the almond is the most beautiful of the fruit trees when in bloom with its large pale pink to white flowers. After flowering, oblong elliptical leaves appear on short spurs. Initially the almond's fuzzy young fruit grows to resemble the closely related peach, but instead of being plump its flesh develops hard green husks. When ripe, the brown outer cover springs open and discharges a shell.

inspiration

Inspiration is everywhere. Look around you in your daily life—and travels—and you will be amazed at the beautiful designs you will see! For many quilters a colorful sunset or exotic blossoms inspire fabric selections or thoughts of appliqué quilts. For me they all become quilting patterns.

I concentrate on finding an intriguing element or motif, simplify the design, then make multiple copies of the final patterns and play with scale and proportion.

design ideas

Quilting patterns are usually flowing lines inspired by a design, not traced and reproduced per se. I consider my cruise line series a souvenir of fun excursions on the Italian Costa and Carnival Cruise Lines, and hereby applaud the designers and manufacturers of their beautiful carpets.

The four continuous-line patterns shown here are named for the wonderful group of quilters on the AQS Caribbean tours: AWESOME, BODACIOUS, CREATIVE, and DELIGHTFUL.

reversed patterns

The easiest way to make a reversed pattern is to photocopy or trace it on one side of paper, then redraw it with an indelible pen. The ink seeps into the back of the paper, providing an accurate reversed image. Or when photocopying, pay a little extra and have a transparent acetate copy made, with an automatic reverse.

AWESOME 3"

BODACIOUS 3"

CREATIVE
2½"

refer to page 66 for longer repeats of each pattern

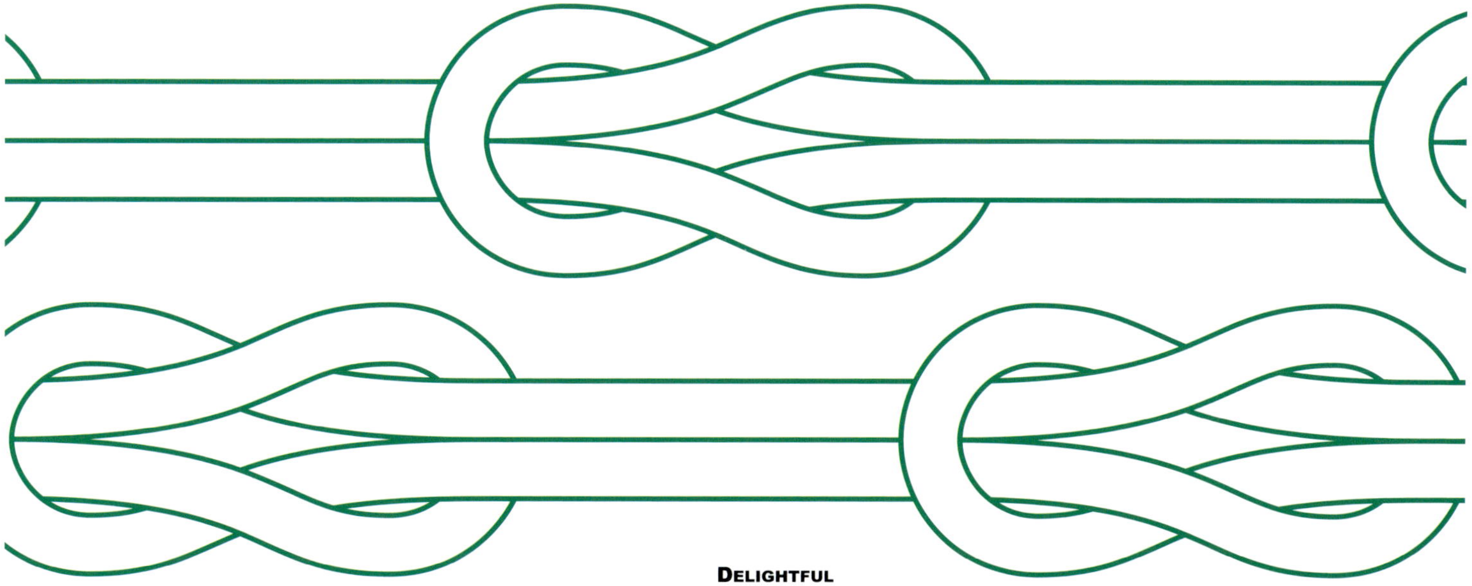

DELIGHTFUL
2½"

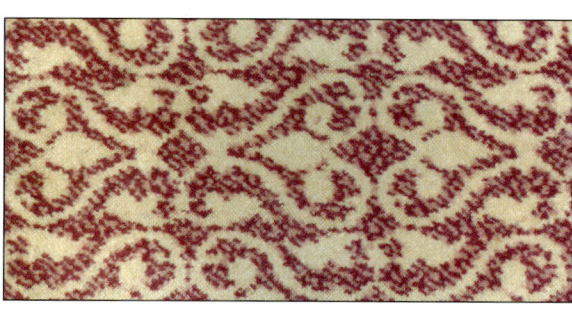

QUILTING UFOS with *Helen's Hints* • Helen Squire

mitered corners

Any pattern can easily be made to turn corners. You will need a reverse of the design to work with. Use liquid correction fluid to cover any unwanted details, shown below as the shaded area. Then retrace on clean paper, make multiple copies, and use the new corner to create a block.

Fold Down

Fold Up

Awesome Maze

QUILTING UFOS with *Helen's Hints* • Helen Squire

AWESOME CENTER

Modify the pattern before marking. Use background freehand textures to emphasize the important elements.

wholecloth quilting

Follow the miter steps on page 67 with any motif to create your own, individual wholecloth design.
Add or omit little details, cut off the shapes as needed, and plan to add textured background areas.

developing a pattern series

Quilt shows and exhibits provide a golden opportunity to try quilting on different types of sit-down and stand-up quilting machines. D.C. DELIGHT was the result of my practicing freehand quilting. It incorporates basic elements of classic continuous-quilting patterns—scroll, teardrop, scallop, and a soft S shape.

design variations

I traced the design I quilted from the fabric onto a napkin, and then made photocopies to play with back in my studio. From the original motif I developed a pantograph, border, block, and a corner variation. Whenever I am happy with a final pattern, I name the series for copyright purposes. Inspired in Chantilly, Virginia, the Washington D.C. series was born!

D.C. DELIGHT REVERSED

D.C. DELIGHT 2½"

D.C. DELIGHT 5"

mitered corners

To miter any pattern you need a reversed copy of the design. Anything can be mitered to create borders and blocks. All the patterns in this series were made using one single motif—D.C. DELIGHT.

WASHINGTON CORNER 2½"

D.C. CORNER 2½"

Spun Sugar

7/8" Square Grid

POTOMAC PANTOGRAPH
3 1/2"

Delightful Sashing

Turkish Delight 6" Circle

QUILTING UFOS with *Helen's Hints* • Helen Squire

Turkish Inspired

Design facing out – TURKISH INSPIRED

Design facing in – TURKISH CROSS

QUILTING UFOS with *Helen's Hints* • Helen Squire

Turkish Cross

2½" Turkish Sashing

QUILTING UFOS with *Helen's Hints* • Helen Squire

77

FLORIDA SUNSET
DOUBLE BORDER

floridian series

Inspiration was a magnificent sunset viewed from Florida's Gulf Coast, and a carved wooden plaque in a St. Petersburg, Florida, restaurant. Once a series is started, I make extra copies and begin planning how to modify the design to improve the quilting.

adaptation

The corners were mitered and reversed at the centers with the patterns touching. This locks in the fullness. Next, the pattern was adapted from traditional to continuous line with both left- and right-facing motifs (see page 80). From one small sketched motif, the entire Floridian series was developed.

applique

Besides using it as a quilting design, this pattern is also perfect for fusible and traditional appliqué, as well as for stenciled quilt tops.

slotted stencils

Most of my designs are sold as slotted stencils—transparent plastic with slashes cut out for tracing. Remember before marking the quilt top to first trace the pattern on paper, remove the stencil, and reconnect the design. Stencils need "bridges" between the slots for manufacturing purposes.

Look at the overall design, and determine if you like its flow. Make extra copies and play with the layout you want, and then "mark" with the stencil.

FLORIDA SUNSET SASHING

GULF COAST

QUILTING UFOS with *Helen's Hints* • Helen Squire

79

Inspired by the curves and straight lines of a storm drain, I developed the continuous pattern MANDY. The many small details were omitted and just the essence of the shape was used.

Actual inspirational photograph

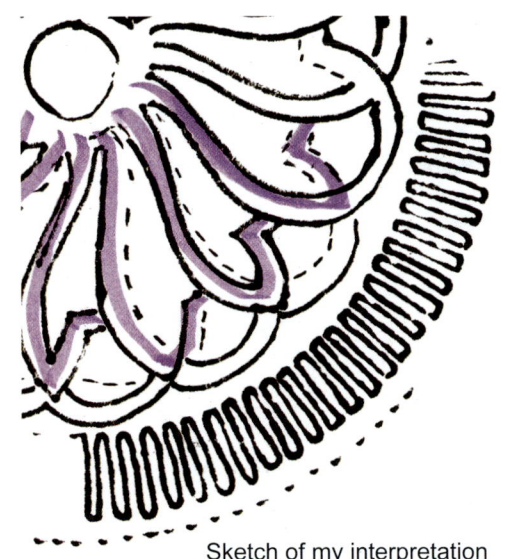

Sketch of my interpretation

medallions

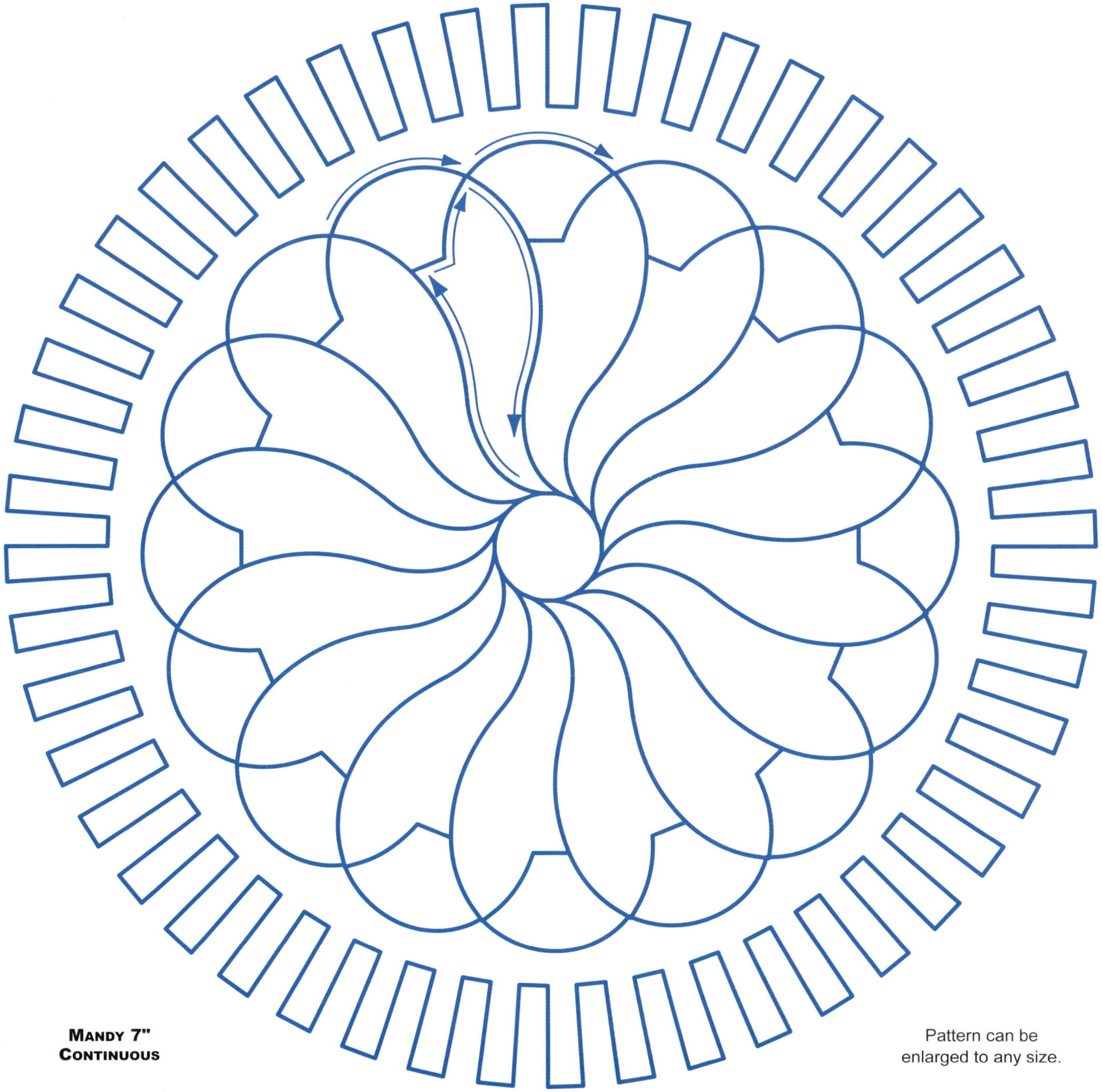

MANDY 7"
CONTINUOUS

Pattern can be enlarged to any size.

QUILTING UFOS with *Helen's Hints* • Helen Squire

circular designs

Medallion-style motifs are always popular at quilt shows yet they have inherent problems for quilters—those wide open areas between the shapes that cause it to "float" in space.

This can best be avoided three ways:
1) Eliminate fussy, smaller details and concentrate on the main design. 2) Enlarge the pattern as big as possible to establish the foreground and minimize the background. 3) Use a filler to flatten the area. Stippling, micro-stitching, straight grid-lines, and McTavishing (swirls) are all good choices.

background fillers

There is a new trend in quilting as freehand fillers are being used to flatten the background to enhance the main design. Remember, the flatter the background area, the "fluffier" the main elements appear. Done right, it almost looks like trapunto—stuffed with extra batting—to raise up the design.

BLACKBURN MEDALLION

QUILTING UFOS with *Helen's Hints* • Helen Squire

Placement Diagram

assembly

Always reconstruct the full repeat of a circular pattern. Make four copies; rotate to connect before planning and marking the quilt, or scan the illustration above and enlarge as needed.

¼ **pattern**
BLACKBURN MEDALLION

Can be enlarged to any size.

Trace, photocopy, or scan. Make multiple copies, rotate, and connect into medallion center. Can be enlarged to any size.

7½"
BLACKBURN SCROLL

QUILTING UFOS with *Helen's Hints* • Helen Squire

**2½" Rose Marie
Continuous Staggered Rows**

from hand to continuous

When adapting designs from hand to machine quilting, keep in mind words like simplify, proportion, and useful sizes. Always eliminate any extra details which can interrupt the stitching flow, and enlarge or reduce the original pattern to meet the size required for your quilting system. The scale of the design will depend on the fabrics used and the quilt top choices—large, medium, or small prints; flannels or plaids; geometric patchwork or floral appliqué; narrow sashing or wide borders, etc.

We all have old quilting pattern collections on paper or plastic. "Practice" is still the best word of all for changing them into designs we can use for today's newer methods of quilting. My pattern Rose Marie appeared in the first *Dear Helen* book—long before pantograph and edge-to-edge became buzz words for quilters. It still looks good over twenty years later.

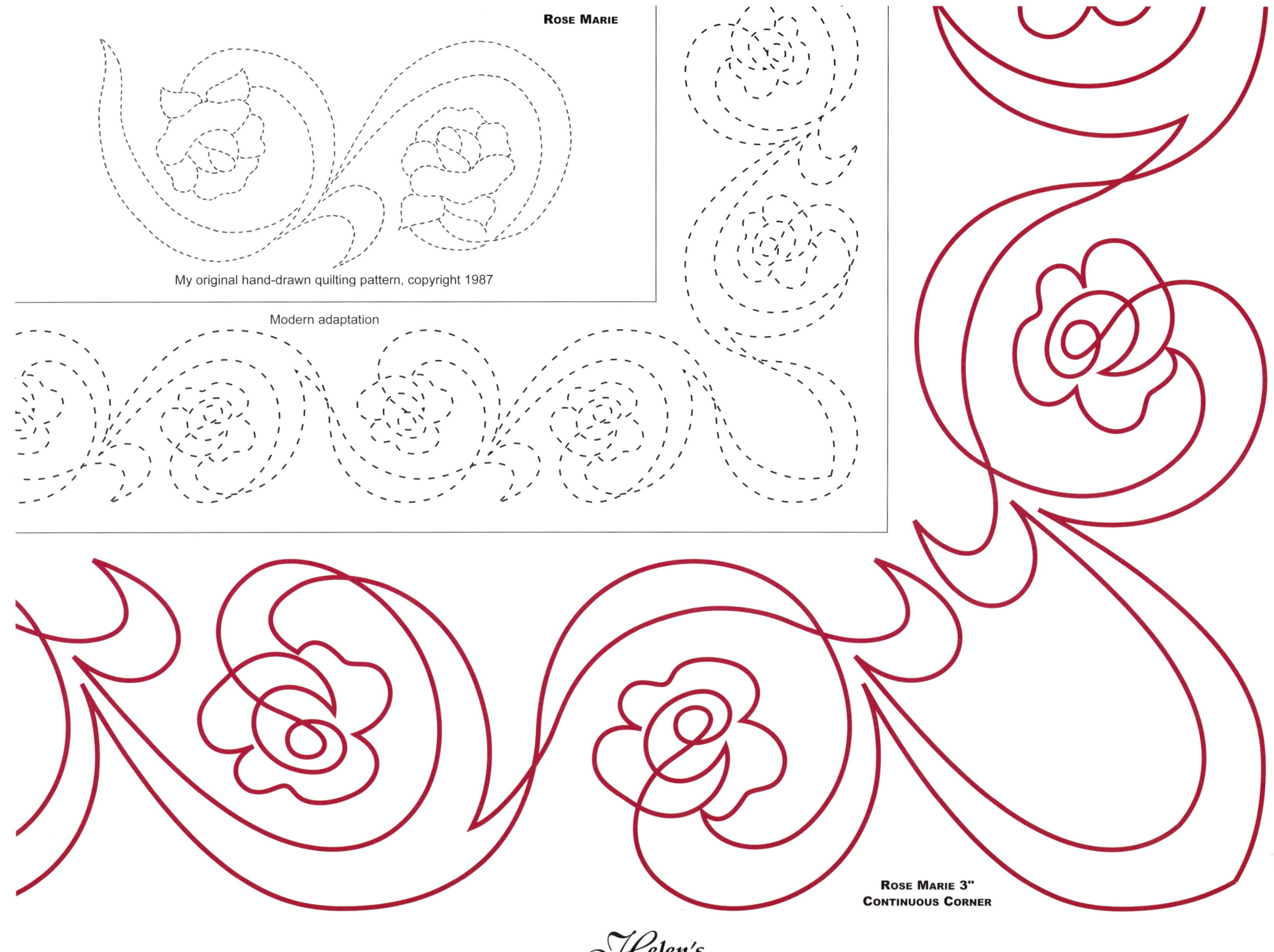

Rose Marie Square

½" Square Grid

QUILTING UFOS with *Helen's Hints* • Helen Squire

ring of roses

There is no up or down to quilting. It is meant to be seen from all four sides. More ecliptic than circular, ROSE MARIE looks good from any direction!

Inspired by a stained-glass dome ceiling, I was fascinated by the fact that a single rose motif could be pivoted ever so slightly to form a new shape.

assembly

To make a full pattern draw a 14" circle (on paper or fabric) as a placement guide to position this quarter-repeat of the design. Copy or trace the pattern and rotate counter-clockwise around the circle. Connect each section with flowing lines and adjust the last curves to fit. Then enlarge to the size you need.

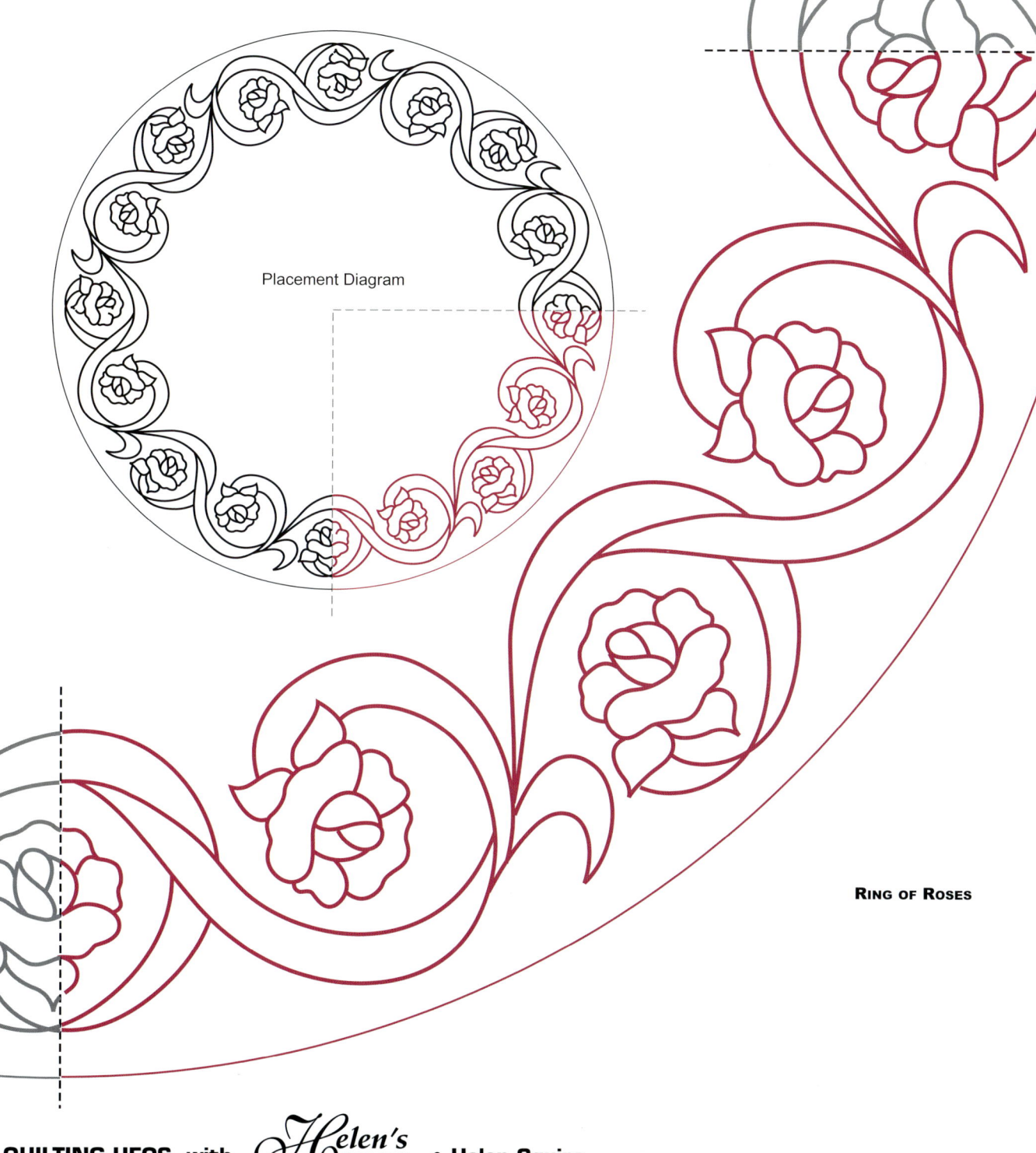

Placement Diagram

RING OF ROSES

worldwide quilting

There are two elements consistent with Zulu quilts: the use of scrap fabrics in a stained-glass motif, and geometric shapes in the native, printed fabrics. The Sweetwaters Quilting Guild of South Africa has introduced a signature style for their quilts.

From the author's collection.

4 Basic Questions...

METHOD OF QUILTING?	Frame machine quilted
TYPE OF BATTING?	Low-loft on rolls
PURPOSE OF PROJECT?	To earn money
THEME OR OCCASION?	Native African design

Solutions

HIGHLIGHTS — An exuberant treatment to a traditional controlled block and technique. The quilting part is secondary to the overall design.

CONCERNS — The pantograph selected should be compatible to the theme of the quilt top. Dainty small flowers are not appropriate.

BENEFITS — Structural quilting is all that is required because the graphic, geometric design is so strong. No marking is necessary.

QUILTING UFOS with *Helen's Hints* • Helen Squire

south africa

As part of a group of humanitarian volunteers who traveled to Kwa Zulu Natal, South Africa, I shared quilting advice and techniques with the Sweetwaters Quilting Guild to help them obtain the skills necessary to support themselves and their families through the sale of their quilts. Professional quilters taught classes in hand, domestic, midarm, and longarm quilting.

The Zulu women and men have a natural talent for color selection, and their quilt designs feature harmonious shades and hues. Our primary mission was to teach universal quilting and design principles, as the students already made precisely pieced tops. The class project I taught could be quilted by hand or machine. By learning hand quilting and finishing, students who had no sewing machine or even electricity in their homes could quilt at home and still earn money.

sponsors

The Rotary Club of Howick and Hilton in South Africa have sponsored the Sweetwaters project since 2003. It is through the International Rotarian efforts and a small mail order catalog that the finished quilts have been sold. A quilt sold for $200 US will feed a family in South Africa for four months.

Elisabeth and Rick Baratta are the enablers of this ongoing endeavor. Elisabeth is the teacher, organizer, supervisor, and tireless promoter of the talents and skills of the quilters.

contacts

For more information please visit Linda Taylor's Web site, www.thequiltingschool.com or contact Elizabeth Baratta at Mzansi Zulu Quilt Centre on the Midland Meander - farm #23, www.quiltsafaris.com. Quilts are marketed locally and to Rotary clubs and quilters in the United States and Canada.

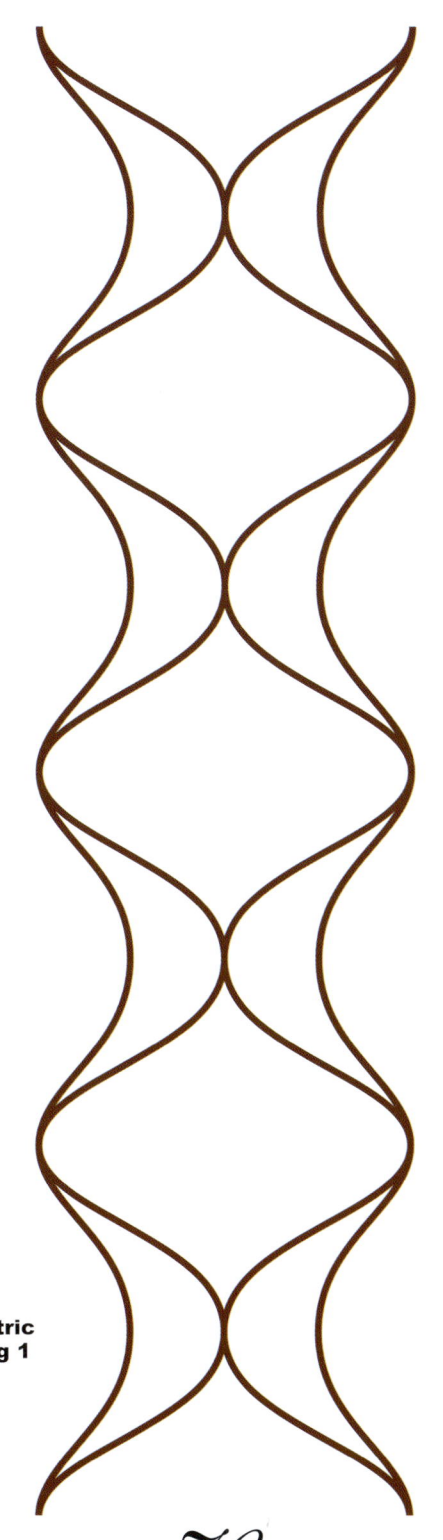

Geometric Sashing 1

Wall quilts made by members of the Sweetwaters Quilting Guild, Zwa Zulu Natal, South Africa.

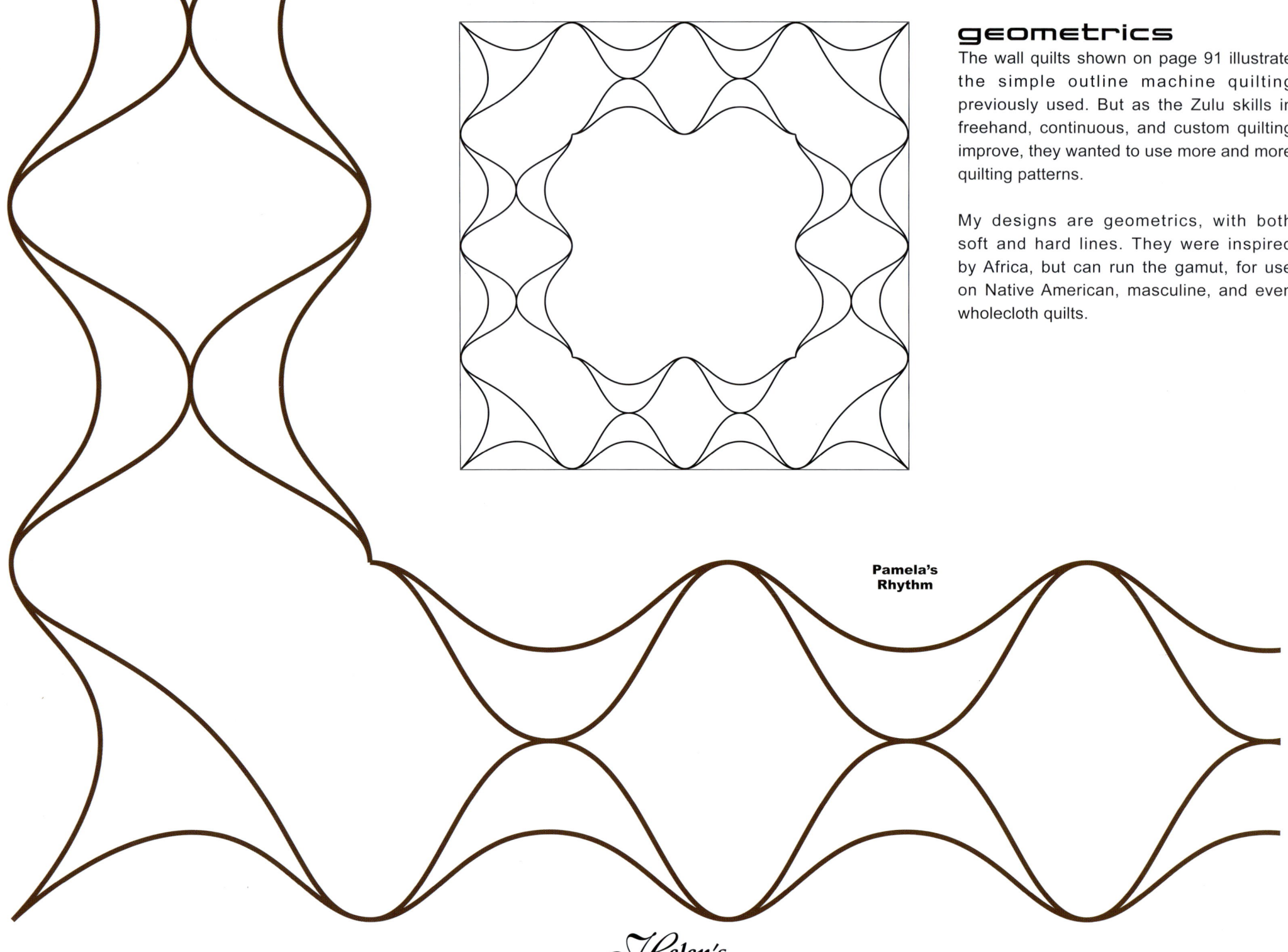

geometrics

The wall quilts shown on page 91 illustrate the simple outline machine quilting previously used. But as the Zulu skills in freehand, continuous, and custom quilting improve, they wanted to use more and more quilting patterns.

My designs are geometrics, with both soft and hard lines. They were inspired by Africa, but can run the gamut, for use on Native American, masculine, and even wholecloth quilts.

Pamela's Rhythm

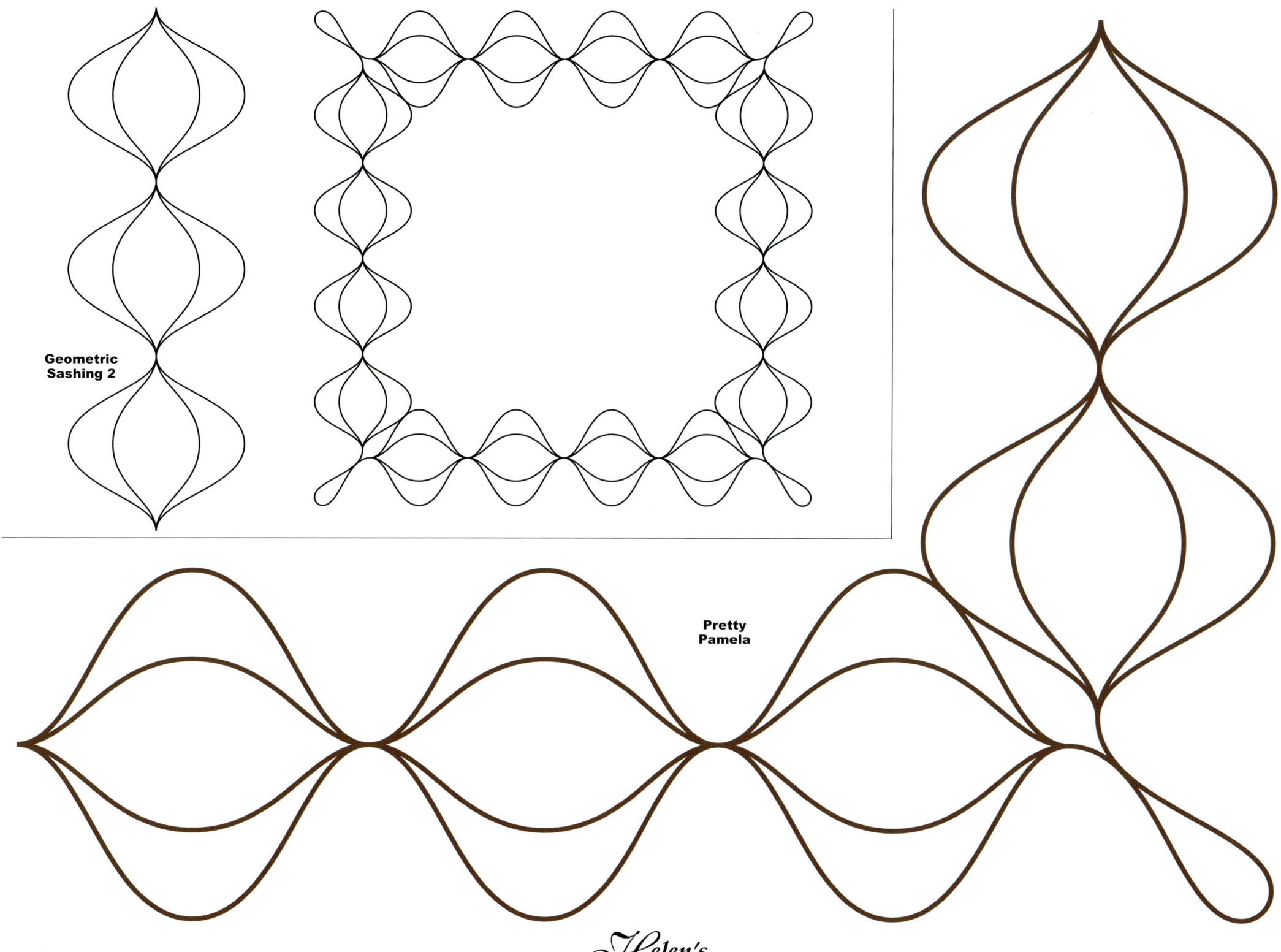

LINDA

HARI

LAUREL

A carved vase was the inspiration, the six variations the result.

JANE

KRISTYN

ELIZABETH

QUILTING UFOS with *Helen's Hints* • Helen Squire

Helen Squire was part of a humanitarian effort of professionals and volunteers who travelled to South Africa to help other quilters. Seated: Helen, Hari Walner, Linda V. Taylor, Elizabeth Baratta, Laurel Barrus. Standing: Julie Matteson, Arlene Jones, John and Carole Smith, Rick Taylor, Georgia Sauter, Todd Fletcher, Jane Sandercock, Kristyn McCoy and Roger Barrus.

Photos by Dr. Des Morrish

about the author

Helen Squire says that when she was asked to join the teaching mission to South Africa with Linda Taylor, Laurel Barrus, and Hari Walner, she asked, "Why me? I'm a traditional hand quilter and you guys are known for longarm, mid-arm, and domestic machine quilting."

The answer was apparent as the trip became a life-altering experience and a reaffirmation of Helen's long-held quilting philosophy and joy of teaching. No matter which method of quilting you use, good design and appropriately selected quilting patterns are what make the difference.

An entrepreneur since 1973 when she started Quilt-In: Lessons • Supplies • Designs, Helen has been an active participant in the growth of the quilt industry as a designer, lecturer, teacher, and television consultant.

Perhaps best known for her *Dear Helen* quilting pattern books—this book is the eighth in the series—she is also the author of *A Quilter's Garden: From Plants of the Holy Land* (see pages 56–63).

Now retired from her position as vice-president of sales and marketing for the American Quilter's Society, she is as busy as ever and still lives in Paducah, Kentucky, Quilt City USA. Lucky her!

Visit her Web site at HelenSquire.com